SCIENCE FUN WITH TOYS

Companion Book by the Author

SCIENCE FUN IN CHICAGOLAND
SECOND EDITION

Describing Over 1,000 Resources,
Including Over 600 from Around the Country

SCIENCE FUN WITH TOYS

A Guide for Parents and Teachers

With Resource Descriptions for
Unique & Educational Toys

THOMAS W. SILLS

Dearborn Resources
P. O. Box 59677
Chicago, IL 60659

Published by Dearborn Resources, P. O. Box 59677, Chicago, IL 60659.

FIRST EDITION   ISBN 0-9644096-2-3

Cover design by Dickinson Associates

Publisher's Cataloging-in-Publication
(Provided by Quality Books, Inc.)

Sills, Thomas W.
       Science fun with toys : a guide for parents and teachers
    : with resource descriptions for unique & educational toys
    / Thomas W. Sills. -- 1st ed.
       p. cm.
       Includes bibliographical references and index.
       ISBN: 0-9644096-2-3
       1. Educational toys--Catalogs. 2. Science--Study and
    teaching--Bibliography--Catalogs. 3. Science--Study and
    teaching--Bibliography--Catalogs--Juvenile literature.
       4. Scientific recreations--Bibliography--Catalogs. I. Title.

    LB1029.T6S54 1999   371.33'0216
                                 QBI99-87

Library of Congress Catalog Card Number: 99-72234

Acknowledgments

Cover Photo of Surf Frogs® printed with permission
of Uncle Milton Industries, Inc. (See page 177)

The companion to this book, *Science Fun in Chicagoland - Second Edition*, was produced during a sabbatical at Wright College, one of the City Colleges of Chicago. The first edition contained a small list of toy sources. During and following this sabbatical this small list expanded into *Science Fun with Toys*. It must be acknowledged that the sabbatical provided an opportunity to start the research for *Science Fun with Toys*.

A countless number of toy company representatives helped with the production of this book. They answered telephone inquires, returned questionnaires, contributed photos and made this book possible. It would be impossible to acknowledge everyone here who openly and freely contributed to the information contained in this book. Thanks! Your efforts will greatly help parents, teachers, students, and science fans who use this book.

vi

Table of Contents

Foreword

"You mean I can take this home?" asks the 4-year-old.

"Yes," says the librarian.
"You may because this is a toy lending library!"

It was the summer of 1934, a time of depression and poverty the United States had not known before. This particular summer a store manager in Los Angeles -- the owner of a dime store -- saw something happen that would form the basis of a new program which would delight children and families the country over. He saw two young boys stealing small toys from his store. Sooner or later the owner realized that these boys were not "bad" boys; they were children without enough money to buy what they wanted to play with.

So this store owner, together with the principal of the boys' school and the probation officer who had made the arrest decided to change things. They organized a toy drive and loaned the collected toys to children in the neighbor-hood. It was this special event that seeded the toy library movement in America. Today the Los Angeles Toy Loan program stands as the oldest and most broad-based toy lending library program in the world -- 25 sites spread through LA. County and more than 10,000 donated toys in circulation.

At the heart of that program, and the toy library program worldwide, is the value of play in the development of every child.

Someone once said, "Play is the child's response to life."

"Play, as we are beginning to understand," writes Lawrence K. Frank in his introduction to the respected early childhood book entitled, *The Complete Book of Children's Play*, "is the way the child learns what no one can teach him. It is the way he explores and orients himself to the actual world of space and time, of things, animals, structures and people. Through play she learns to live in our symbolic world of meanings and values, of progressive striving for deferred goals, at the same time exploring and experimenting and learning in her own individualized way.

"Through play," Frank continues, "the child practices and rehearses endlessly the complicated and subtle patterns of human living and communication and experiences."

Child expert Dr. Robert M. Goldenson, coauthor of the same book, comments that "the play life of children and adults cannot simply be left to take care of itself...To get the maximum benefit from recreation, it has to be planned wisely and geared to interests, abilities and above all to growth...There are many forms of play, and many facilities that can be provided only by the community at large. For a full life of play, there must be not only fun in the family but fun on the town. And don't think that play-planning is needed for the underprivileged only. It is needed for all!"

As if a fruition of that thought, toy lending libraries developed as a community response to a recognized need for play experiences, an awareness that has increased substantively in the latter half of this century. The first settings -- schools, public libraries and Head Start programs--had the families and financial resources necessary to support toy loan. Today the sites have expanded, yet still are anchored to programs that serve children -- child care centers, hospitals, social service agencies, in addition to schools and public libraries. The educators and other professionals working with children in these settings are still striking out for toy libraries today. They have created different models that share the elements of toys and toy loan. Though they may differ in context and procedures, toy lending libraries respond to the basic play

X

needs of childhood, are child centered, offer play space and toy loan guided by professionals. They are also, for the most part, not-for-profit enterprises.

Of Many Shapes, Sizes

"A youngster comes into the children's department of the Glenview Public Library, grabs a jigsaw puzzle from a shelf of toys and announces that he wants to take it home.

"Instead of telling him that he may play with the puzzle only at the library, the head children's librarian takes his name and lets him check it out for a week," says the story in a local Evanston, Ill., newspaper about the children's department in the Glenview library which houses some 700 toys. "People in the community really appreciate it and see it as an extension of their tax money," says the head children's librarian.

The Brooklyn Branch of the Cuyahoga County (Ohio) Public Library System houses 1,300 toys in its six-year-old facility, the brain child of Brooklyn Mayor John C. Coyne, who built the toy library as part of a new multi-million dollar public library several years ago. Here toys are used in reading circles and parent education programs in addition to being offered for loan.

Toy lending also transpires on wheels. In a typical mobile lending situation, the toys circulate to more widespread, often rural and sometimes economically depressed areas of a community. The program scope may include five or six counties. One venerated mobile program established in 1972, The Rainbow Fleet in Oklahoma City, Ok., circulates materials in three vans to licensed family day care homes. Offered in conjunction with the 3,000 toys in circulation are monthly education classes on child development for the providers, who are interested in skills that relate to a wide-ranging group of children from birth to age 8 or 10. The educational programs of Rainbow Fleet and many other toy lending centers have become part-n-parcel to their success.

Toy Libraries Help Children With More Specialized Learning Needs

As much as toy lending came about in response to educators' needs, toy loan was also arrived at because of a deficiency of play opportunities for children with special needs. In fact, the European movement of toy libraries, which preceded the development of toy lending in America by 20 years (with the exception of the L.A. Toy Loan Program), was borne of Swedish mothers with children whose physical abilities limited their play. It was again the needs of these children and their families -- together with a few dedicated and entrepreneurial women in America -- that gave rise to the Lekotek movement in the United States in the early '80s.

Lekotek is a Swedish word that loosely translated means play library. From one lekotek in Evanston begun in the early '80s has evolved the National Lekotek Center, now a network of 60+ lekoteks in the Western hemisphere, principally in the U.S., providing support and services to children with special needs and their families. Lekoteks take shape as resource and play centers, and many also house Compuplay centers that offer family computer play programs and loan adaptive software to visitors. The National Lekotek Center has adapted the slogan, Lekotek...leading the way for accessible play. Its three-part mission is *to demonstrate innovative practices that promote learning-oriented play within families of children with disabilities ... to contribute to the knowledge bank about the link between play and early learning for children with special needs... and to disseminate an accumulated learning about play, toys, technology and family support to critical audiences that need and want to know*. The national center provides leadership training for Lekotek teachers, camps for special needs children in addition to a year-round individualized program of play visits for families with disabled and at-risk children.

The Lekotek program, like most toy lending libraries, engenders praise and loyalty from all visitors. Says one Lekotek parent, "When you have a child with disabilities, lots of decisions come down to what you can afford. One of the great things about Lekotek is that you can try out toys without thinking about whether you can afford to buy them."

The economic advantage of all these play centers, whether tailored especially for disabled children or open to the public-at-large, is not lost on parents, educators or providers. The toys housed in a toy library offer fun and educational value and are able to withstand repeat usage. Bikes, trikes and climbing toys will exercise large-motor skills, while pull toys, construction toys, balls, games, puzzles, etc, stimulate small motor skills. These products can be expensive and draw heavily on a family's budget. Among a variety of publications, you will find the USA Toy Library Association repeatedly mentioned in the newspaper *The Tightwad Gazette*. Appropriately so. The toy library offers an economical option to out-of-pocket expenditures.

Toy libraries also serve as a testing laboratories. All too often the product that is appealing today will become unpopular a short while later. The toy library allows children to experiment, and gives parents and providers added confidence when finally making personal toy purchases.

Daily Operation: Toy Libraries Create Good Citizens

With their dependence on the return of toys in good working condition, toy libraries encourage values of honesty and fair play. The L.A. Toy Loan publishes an honor code: Toy loan members are: Courteous, Patient, Wait Their Turn, Honest, Take Care of Toys, Encourage and Help Each Other, and Always Return Toys. The honor borrower receives a certificate and special toy from a chest that houses new toys to be given in reward for exemplary behavior. All toy libraries subscribe to the honor code, and in fact it works. Although a toy library may fine for missing toys or parts, this is in reality more of a nuisance than a problem.

The care and maintenance of toys fall to the toy librarian and her helpers, who must follow health codes of cleanliness. Whether a toy is loaned for a week or a month is the decision of the local toy library. How a toy is exhibited -- whether displayed in translucent or mesh bags on shelves in the public area or displayed in photo albums and retrieved by the toy librarian at the request of the visitor -- varies from center to center.

Staffing also runs the gambit, with most toy libraries managed by a combination of employee and volunteer staff. Usually an early childhood development background gives the chief staff officer secure footing in the development and implementation process.

Best Kept Secret: Spreading Awareness of Toy Libraries

Toy lending libraries are a "best kept secret." While their existence may be well known to their patrons, the general public is often unfamiliar with them. Increasing the awareness of toy libraries is a core concern of the USA Toy Library Association (USA-TLA), a 14-year-old not-for-profit organization headquartered in Evanston, Ill.

The USA-TLA started with 15 people who were involved in toy libraries in the United States. Before their initial meeting these educators were operating in isolation. As a new entity, the group wanted to build a network of communication and cooperation to stimulate the growth of toy libraries in the U.S.A. They were united in the belief that the experience of play in early childhood influences the quality of life for the adult. They all felt that play and toys should become priorities in early childhood programs throughout the country.

The corps of 15 were also united by a strong international tie: the "seasoned" toy library movement overseas and in Canada. England, Sweden, Denmark, Japan and most other countries in the free world foster -- even support -- toy libraries. The global reach of toy loan is manifest in the International Toy Library Association, a 20+-year-old entity that sponsors a conference every three years. Fifty-two countries are members, representing thousands of toy lending programs throughout the world. USA-TLA directors guided the formation of the International Association and continue to support it.

These entrepreneurial Americans went on to build a national program that now identifies close to 300 toy libraries in 37 of the United States, with Illinois and California leading the way. Some operate as centers of support and learning for families that have a special-needs child; some operate for the general public as toy corners in the public library; some support hospitalized children; others reach into the community through school systems, and others stand alone as independent community services.

Wherever they exist, toy libraries usually are grass-roots organizations designed by the communities they serve. For that very reason, USA-TLA has sponsored -- and continues to sponsor -- conferences all over the United States. These programs provide extended networking opportunities and educational advantage for somewhat disparate toy librarians. Typically conferences boast speakers of national import, renowned for work with children, toys and play. Joanne Oppenheim, Rhoda Redleaf, Julie Creighton, Susan Myers and others are some of the leading speakers at national events. Smaller roundtable sessions take place annually and allow for ample give-and-take among attendees.

The USA-TLA also supports these toy librarians by providing information on toy library management, toys, play and child development. We put them in touch with each other and draw out the experts for advice and counsel. The USA-TLA's new Web site -- **www.sjdccd.cc.ca.us/toylibrary** -- offers visitors the opportunity to find the closest toy library to their home or base of operation.

Every day the USA Toy Library Association responds to queries about the closest toy lending library, questions from parents, teachers and others. Building awareness of toy libraries and supporting the individuals and institutions that wish to develop toy loan centers is the first mission of the USA-TLA.

A close second to recommend quality toys for the toy library. USA-TLA is asked repeatedly where to find quality toys. Tom Sills, in his extensive work with toy makers based all over the world, supplies an answer in this guide to exemplary toy products which emphasize science learning through play. By perusing the pages of this book, you will learn how to effectively expand your science program for all ages of children.

If you have interest in becoming involved in toy libraries, please write USA-TLA, 2530 Crawford Ave., Evanston, IL 60201 - Ste. 111, or e-mail us at usatla@aol.com.

-- **Judith Q. Iacuzzi**
Executive Director
USA Toy Library Association
www.sjdccd.cc.ca.us/toylibrary

Judith Quayle Iacuzzi has served as executive director of the USA Toy Library Association since 1984, the year it was founded. Since then, the program of toy lending libraries in the United States has quadrupled, 10 national and regional conferences and five international toy library conferences have been held on the subject of toy lending, play and early childhood development. Judy earned her masters from the Medill School of Journalism at Northwestern University where she also earned her bachelor's degree. She and her husband Tony live with their three children Elizabeth, Franny and David in Evanston, Illinois.

Judith Q. Iacuzzi

Tips on How to Locate Toys For Sale

◆ First, see Web sites to learn if a manufacturer or distributor sells individual toys via retail mail order, learn whether a toy you want is available, or if the manufacturer offers newer toys.

◆ Telephone and ask toy sources in this guide for a catalog of their products. Understand that a few toy sources reserve catalogs for only toy store buyers or schools.

◆ Do not expect the person who answers the telephone to be able to answer your question. Ask to speak to someone who can answer questions about toys or questions about where their toys are for sale.

◆ Do not expect large manufacturers to know retail stores selling their toys. Ask these large manufacturers for the name and telephone number of a local distributor that sells to stores in your area. These distributors can tell you where to buy the toy.

◆ Understand that toy distributors, commonly known as the "middle man," may or may not sell individual toys to the public. Just ask.

◆ Telephone your local retail toy store to see if the toy you want is available. Show this book to someone at your local retail toy store. Perhaps the store can special order the toy you want.

◆ Understand that toy buyers for retail stores do not always know what to buy, because these buyers do not always know what the public wants. When they make informed choices, their store will be more successful.

◆ Do not expect a toy to be available forever. Availability depends on market demand and production quantity.

◆ Have fun!

Dedicated to

Learners at Play Everywhere

SCIENCE FUN WITH TOYS

Chapter

1

Arts & Crafts for Science

A G INDUSTRIES

Contact Aaron Tibbs   15335 N E 95th St, Redmond, WA 98052 800-233-7174 425-885-4599 Fax 425-885-4672 Email atibbs@whitewings.com http://www.whitewings.com Manufacturer Retail and Wholesale (Elementary School to High School) Ask for 12-page catalog. Educational kits for constructing paper airplane gliders, boats and origami. Whitewings series includes the History of Passenger Planes, Future of Flight,

Whitewings® Science of Flight Photo Courtesy of A G Industries

History of Jet Fighters, Racers, Space Shuttle, Science of Flight. Display cases for home and retail stores.

CALIFORNIA PACIFIC DESIGNS
P O Box 2660, Alameda, CA 94501 510-521-7914 Fax 510-865-0851
Manufacturer Wholesale (Elementary School)
Ask for brochures. Manufacturer of stickers and craft kits about animals from nature: Earthwing Collector Stickers, Tin & Craft Kits, Mini Wood Craft Puzzles, and Glass Paperweights.

DOWLING MAGNETS
**Contact JoAnn Chew   P O Box 1829, Sonoma, CA 95476
800-624-6381 707-935-0352 Fax 707-935-1231
Email dowling@DowlingMagnets.com Manufacturer   Wholesale
(High School to Adult)**
Magnets and magnetic materials of numerous shapes and dimensions for educational use. Ask for catalog.

FAMILY GAMES INC.
**P O Box 97, Snowdon, Montreal, Canada H3X-3T3 800-291-1176
514-485-1834   Fax 514-485-2944   Manufacturer   Wholesale
(Elementary School)**
Ask for 18-page catalog. Educational games, puzzles, and activities. Science products include MoonDust (paint natures creatures with colored powder), Too Cool Kit Mad Scientist Party, Tantrix award-winning puzzles, and more.

FRANCIS FAMILY TOYS LTD.

1314 Rufina Circle #A9, Santa Fe, NM 87505 505-473-4501 Fax 505-473-4519 Manufacturer Wholesale (Elementary School) Ask for brochure. Manufacturer of CREATEures, stuffed cotton animals that you paint. Also, heirloom quality folk toys including Jacob's Ladder, Tie Dye Kit, and preschool wooden toys.

CREATEures -Paint a Friend
Photo Courtesy of Francis Family Toys

GEOCENTRAL

Contact Cindy Vader   1721 Action Ave, Napa, CA 94559 800-231-6083 707-224-7500 Fax 707-224-7400 Email cindy@geocentral.com Manufacturer Wholesale (Elementary School to High School) Quantity sets of rocks and minerals for retail sale. Flat boxes of mineral and fossil assortments. Sea shell glow night lights. Agate bookends. Twenty four-page catalog.

"I Made My...Kaleidoscope" Kit
Photo Courtesy of Homecrafters

HOMECRAFTERS MANUFACTURING

1859 Kenion Point, Snellville, GA 30078   770-985-5460
Fax 770-978-3012
Email   hmctoys@aol.com
http://homecrafters-mfg.com
Manufacturer Wholesale and Retail (Elementary School)
Ask for brochure describing "I Made My...Periscope!" kit and "I Made My...Kaleidoscope!" kit and other Home Crafted Toys.

Magnetic Play Board
Photo Courtesy of Huntar Co.

HUNTAR CO. INC.

Contact Tammy Lawrence   473 Littlefield Ave, So. San Francisco, CA 94080 800-566-8686
650-873-8282   Fax 650-873-8292
Email
Huntar.Magnet@worldnet.att.net
Manufacturer   Wholesale (Elementary School to High School)
Ask for 24-page catalog. Magnetic products include activity kits, wands, marbles, chips, shaped magnets, puzzle wheels, math & letter wheels, play boards, and floating rings.

INSECT LORE
P O Box 1535, Shafter, CA 93263 800-LIVE-BUG 805-746-6047
Fax 805-746-0334 Email insect@lightspeed.net
http://www.insectlore.com **Manufacturer Wholesale Retail Mail
Order (Elementary School)**
Ask for 32-page catalog. Distributor of many science kits and books on
nature's creatures, including ant farms, butterflies, insects, plants & trees,
science project ideas, frogs and amphibians, and nature videos.

JCS, INC.
P O Box 12455, Chicago, IL 60612 800-469-6653 312-226-5772
**Fax 312-226-5774 Manufacturer Distributor Wholesale
(Elementary School to Adult)**
Ask for brochure. Voyage Earth labs include Volcano Adventure,
Earthquake Explorer, Tornado Adventure, and Geyser Exploration.
Weird Monster Science includes Shrink Putty, Power Surge, Rocket
Flight Formula, Invisible Ink, Flying Things and Slime Conversion
Potion. Crafty Kids series includes Foot Prints, Scribble, and Face Kit.

KRISTAL EDUCATIONAL INC.
**Distributed by Ira Cooper, Inc., P O Box 2137, Woodinville, WA
98072 206-720-6264 Fax 206-720-6317**
http://www.mysteriousart.com **Distributor Wholesale
(Elementary School to High School)**
Ask for 26-page catalog. Mineral crystal growing kits, including Space
Age Crystal Kits; Crystal Spheres, Pyramids & Jewelry; Crystal Caves;
Dab'a'Dino (Paintable stuffed dinosaurs); National Geographic Society's
Expedition Series; Gem Tree Kits; Archeology Kits; and more.

MRS. GROSSMAN'S PAPER CO.

Contact Jeff Shaw   3810 Cypress Drive, Petaluma, CA 94954
800-457-4570 707-763-1700 Fax 707-763-7121
Email jshaw@mrsgrossmans.com http://www.mrsgrossmans.com
Manufacturer Wholesale (Elementary School)
Ask for 74-page catalog. Peel-off stickers, idea books, and kits include topics on dinosaurs, nature, ocean life, and animals.

NATUREPRINT PAPER PRODUCTS

P. O. Box 314, Moraga, CA 94556 Manufacturer
(Elementary School to High School)
Natureprint paper and transparencies. This sun-sensitive paper exposes in direct sunlight to create white on blue prints of leaf outlines or animal picture transparencies. Expose for 2-3 minutes and then develop in tap water in seconds.

PARALLEL UNIVERSE CORPORATION

Flying Saucer

Swan

Patterns for Cardboard Toys
Photo Courtesy of Parallel Universe

2201 Deschenes St, Ottawa, Ontario, Canada   K2B 6N2   888-877-5556
613-761-7658   Fax 613-722-4750
Email   parallel@magi.com
http://www.magi.com/~parallel
Manufacturer   Distributor
Wholesale   Retail   Mail Order
(Preschool to Elementary School)
Ask for brochure.   This company designs print tissue paper patterns, similar to dress patterns, that are traced over cardboard boxes to create children's toys. Patterns include flying saucer, tug boat, castle, treasure chest, and more.

PATAIL ENTERPRISES, INC.

27324 Camino Capistrano #129, Laguna Niguel, CA 92677 800-9900-TOY 714-367-0530 Fax 714-367-0138 Manufacturer Wholesale (Elementary School) Ask for brochures. Craft sets. Art & Science Projects include Light Show Lamp and Waterfall Garden.

Light Show Lamp Kit
Photo Courtesy of Patail Enterprises

PEELEMAN-MCLAUGHLIN ENTERPRISES INC.

European Expressions, 4153 South 300 West, Murray, UT 84107 800-779-2205 Fax 801-263-2053 Manufacturer Wholesale Retail Mail Order http://www.europeanexpressions.com (Elementary School) Ask for brochure. Science toys include Perfume Creations, Magnetic Intelligence Test, and Magnetic Fishing.

Perfume Creations
Photo Courtesy of
Peeleman-McLaughlin Enterprises

Growth Chart Poster
Photo Courtesy of Pigment & Hue

PIGMENT & HUE, INC.

Contact Howard Kurtz 8730-I Santa Monica Blvd, West Hollywood, CA 90069 800-850-8221 310-855-9581 Fax 310-855-9671 Manufacturer Wholesale (Elementary School)
Ask for 16-page catalog. Cards for kids to color combining art and science. They include place mats, posters, and Banners. Science products: Explore the Universe, Games at the Museum, Angelfish & Butterflyfish, Parrots, Tulips, Dinosaur Pals, Endangered Animals, and more.

PLAYWERKS, INC.

4405 Engle Road, Fort Wayne, IN 46804 800-598-7470 219-432-5328 Fax 219-432-5461 http://www.playwerkstoys.com Manufacturer Wholesale (Elementary School)
Ask for brochure. Reusable stick-on figures activity sets with play board include Space Station, Ocean Adventure, Dinosaurs, and more.

SENTOSPHERE USA

81 E Second St, New York, NY 10003 212-674-8202
Fax 212-505-9526 Manufacturer Wholesale (Elementary School)
Ask for brochure. Products include Follow Your Nose (a game with 30 distinct aroma samples), Perfume Maker (chemically create more than 100 different fragrances), and many preschool wood puzzles of nature and science.

THE STRAIGHT EDGE, INC.
296 Court Street, Brooklyn, NY 11231 800-732-3628 718-643-2794
Fax 718-403-9582 Email straedge@aol.com Manufacturer
(Preschool to Elementary School)
Ask for 12-page catalog. Products include Color a Magnet and Read a
Mat (table mat) with animals, math, and science.

TESSELATIONS
688 W 1st St, Suite 5, Tempe, AZ
85281 800-655-5341 602-967-7455
Fax 602-967-7582
Email tessella@futureone.com
http://tesselations.com
Manufacturer Wholesale
Retail Mail Order
(Elementary School to Adult)
Ask for 8-page catalog. Puzzles that
creatively combine math, art and fun,
including Monkey Business; Spin,
Rock & Roll, a 3-D puzzle that creates
tops, pendulums, balls, and more;

Tetrominoes
Photo Courtesy of Tesselations

Tessel-Gons; Tessel-Gon Stars; Tessellation Kaleidoscope; Tangrams;
Captured Worlds, panoramic projections on polyhedra; and many more.
Classroom kits available.

Biocolor Paint Set
Photo Courtesy of University Games

UNIVERSITY GAMES CORP.
1633 Adrian Road, Burlingame, CA 94101 650-692-2500
Fax 650-692-2770 Manufacturer (Elementary School)
Ask for catalog. Toys available include Great Explorations, Raintree Puzzles, SlideMaster, Biocolor Paint Set, and more.

Chapter

2

Books

References about Toys

AMERICAN SPECIALTY TOY RETAILING ASSOCIATION (ASTRA)

Janet Koerner, Executive Director 206 Sixth Ave, Suite 900, Des Moines, IA   50309 515-282-8192   Fax 515-282-9117   Telephone 888-303-TOYS to locate toys at participating retailers.
Email astra@astratoy.org   http://www.astratoy.org (Reference)
This Association consists of 800 members, including retailers, manufacturers, manufacturer's representatives, and industry-related members. ASTRA's web site has Toy Store Finder that locates retail stores near you, articles of interest for parents, and linkages for parents and kids.

EARTH-FRIENDLY TOYS

by George Pfiffner John Wiley & Sons, Inc., New York   1994
128 pages $ 12.95 (Reference)
This book describes how to make toys and games from reusable objects.
One learns recycling while making fun mechanical action science toys.

EXPLORING MATTER WITH TOYS

Terrific Science Press, Miami University Middletown, 4200 East
University Blvd, Middletown, OH 45042 513-424-4444
http://www.muohio.edu/~ccecwis/ 1995 224 pages Grades 1-4
($19.95 NSTA 800-722-NSTA) ($ 19.95 Showboard 800-323-9189)
(Reference)
Uses inexpensive, familiar and easily obtainable play materials to
understand the senses and matter. Developed with the support of the
National Science Foundation.

GET TOYS ON THE INTERNET

http://www.gettoys.com (Reference)
Toys for sale over the Internet.

INVESTIGATING SOLIDS, LIQUIDS, AND GASES WITH TOYS

Terrific Science Press, Miami University Middletown, 4200 East
University Blvd, Middletown, OH 45042 513-424-4444
http://www.muohio.edu/~ccecwis/ 1995 298 pages Grades 6-8
($19.95 NSTA 800-722-NSTA) ($ 19.95 Showboard 800-323-9189)
(Reference)
Uses inexpensive, familiar and easily obtainable play materials to
understand states of matter and changes of state. Developed with the
support of the National Science Foundation.

NEWTON'S TOY BOX GUIDE

Delta Education, P O Box 915, Hudson, NH   03051-0915
800-258-1302 (During office hours.)   Fax   603-880-6520
http://www.delta-ed.com $ 27.95 (Reference)
The classroom kit, Newton's Toy Box, for grades 6-8, uses toys to teach science concepts of force, mass, velocity, gravity and acceleration. Complete kit with toys $ 369.00

SCIENCE FARE

by Wendy Saul Harper & Row, Publishers, New York   1986
Paperback, 295 pages Out of print. (Reference)
This classic reference book is an illustrated guide and catalog of toys, books and activities about science for kids. The first nine chapters discuss science education for parents and teachers and the last eleven chapters describe specific resources by subject. Introduction by Isaac Asimov.

TEACHING CHEMISTRY WITH TOYS

Terrific Science Press, Miami University Middletown, 4200 East University Blvd, Middletown, OH 45042   513-424-4444
http://www.muohio.edu/~ccecwis/ 1995   296 pages   Ages 5-14
($19.95 NSTA 800-722-NSTA) ($ 19.95 Showboard 800-323-9189)
(Reference)
Uses inexpensive, familiar and easily obtainable play materials. Developed with the support of the National Science Foundation.

TEACHING PHYSICS WITH TOYS
Terrific Science Press, Miami University Middletown, 4200 East
University Blvd, Middletown, OH 45042 513-424-4444
http://www.muohio.edu/~ccecwis/ 1995 296 pages Grades K-9
($19.95 NSTA 800-722-NSTA) ($ 19.95 Showboard 800-323-9189)
(Reference)
Uses inexpensive, familiar and easily obtainable play materials.
Developed with the support of the National Science Foundation.

TOYS IN SPACE:
EXPLORING SCIENCE WITH THE ASTRONAUTS
by Dr. Carolyn Sumners, Project Director for the Toys in Space
Program, NASA McGraw-Hill, 11 West 19th Street, New York, NY
10011 800-822-8158 1997 512 pages $ 29.95
(800-722-NSTA $ 29.95) (Reference)
Many mechanical action toys were taken on a NASA shuttle mission to
observe their motion in weightless space. These toys, how they move on
Earth, and what happened to them in space are described.

Toys & Books for Children

ACCORD PUBLISHING, LTD.
1407 Larimer St, Suite 206, Denver, CO 80202 888-333-1676
303-595-3839 Fax 303-595-4436 Manufacturer Retail Mail Order
(Elementary School to High School)
Ask for catalog. Publisher of award winning Eyeball Animation Series
of Children's Books on science subjects and the annual Weather Guide
Calendar.

ANDY VODA OPTICAL TOYS

RR 5, #387, Brattleboro, VT 05301 Tel/Fax 802-254-6115 Email avoda@together.net http://www.together.net/~avoda/optical.htm/ Manufacturer Retail (All ages)

Ask for brochure. Phenakistascope with six magic wheels, Thaumatrope, Couples spinning pictures, Flipbooks, Greeting Flipbooks, Make-it-yourself Zoetrope.

CHILD'S PLAY

Contact Joe Gardner 67 Minot Ave, Auburn, ME 04210 800-472-0099 Fax 800-854-6989 973-731-3777 Fax 973-731-3740 cplay@mail.idt.net Manufacturer (Preschool to Elementary School)

Ask for 24-page catalog. Books, toys and games include Time Tunnel, Bats, Spiders, Children of the Sun (Astronomy), Metamorphoses (Butterflies and Frogs), Sorting and Matching, Shape and Color, Arithmetic Games, and more.

EDC PUBLISHING

10302 E 55th Place #B, Tulsa, OK 74146-6515 / P O Box 470663, Tulsa, OK 74146-6515 800-475-4522 918-622-4522 Fax 918-655-7919 http://www.edcpub.com Manufacturer Wholesale (Elementary School)

Creepy Crawlies Kid Kit
Photo Courtesy of EDC Publishing

Ask for Usborne Books catalog. Kids Kits contain a book and specially selected age-appropriate materials. Kids Kits include science products: Dinosaurs, Nature, At the Seaside, Dinosaurs Picture History, Science with Air, Things that Fly, Science with Magnets, Paper Planes, Batteries & Magnets, Science Experiments, Young Naturalist, and more.

EDUCATIONAL INSIGHTS

Contact Customer Service Department 16941 Keegan Ave, Carson, CA 90746 800-995-4436 310-884-2000 Fax 800-995-0506 Email service@edin.com http://www.edin.com **Manufacturer Retail and Wholesale (Elementary School)**

Ask for 32-page catalog. GeoSafari computer games, Mini-Museums, Mystery Rock, Exploring Ecology, Natural Collections, Mysteries of Light, Mysteries of Magnetism, Adventures in Science series has 12 different projects, Science Safari Stickers, Fantastic Cards on science subjects, Animal Big Books 14" x 20", Bug Viewers, Dino Checkers, Dino Tic Tac Toe.

FELDSTEIN & ASSOCIATES INC.

1946 N 13th St, Toledo, OH 43624 419-242-6500 Fax 419-242-5939 **Distributor Wholesale (Elementary School)**

Ask for brochure. Distributor of The Singing Bird Book with 12 of the most recognized bird songs at the touch of a button.

JUMP START DEVELOPMENTAL PLAY PRODUCTS
Contact Aubrey Carton Belle Curve Records, Inc., P O Box 18387,
Boulder, CO 80308 888-357-5867 303-494-7540 Fax 303-494-7555
Email at http://www.hopskipjumpstart.com http://bellecurve.com
Manufacturer Distributor Wholesale
(Preschool and Elementary School)
Ask for brochure. Tapes, CDs and parent-friendly books introduce kids
with sensory-motor, developmental, and social-emotional challenges.

KLUTZ
455 Portage Ave, Palo Alto, CA
94306-2213 800-558-8944
Fax 800-524-4075 650-424-0739
Manufacturer Retail Mail Order
(Elementary School to High School)
Ask for the 46-page Klutz Catalogue.
Really fun toys and novelties. Amazon
Worms, Smartballs, Smartrings, The
Explorabook - a kids science museum
in a book, ExploraCenter, Backyard
Weather Station kit, Mega-Magnet Set,
Backyard Bird Book with bird caller,
The Aerobie Orbiter, Rubber Stamp
Bug Kit, Vinyl Vermin, Kids

**Klutz Explorabook
A Science Museum in a Book**
Photo Courtesy of Klutz

Gardening Guide, World Record Paper Airplane Kit, The Arrowcopter,
Megaballoons, Bubble Book, Zoetrope, juggling materials.

KOLBE CONCEPTS, INC.

P. O. Box 15667, Phoenix, AZ 85060 602-840-9770 Fax 602-952-2706
http://www.kolbe.com Manufacturer Retail (All ages)
Ask for brochure. Think-ercises, Glop Shop - inventor's assortment, Go
Power - science experiments, Using Your Senses, Solar Power Winners
- experiment book, Decide & Design - inventor's book.

LAWRENCE HALL OF SCIENCE

University of California, Berkeley, CA 94720-5200 510-642-1016
Fax 510-642-1055 Email lhsstore@uclink4.berkeley.edu
http://www.lhs.berkeley.edu
See web site filled with books, teachers' and parents' guides, science kits,
videos, and ordering instructions. Known as Eureka!: Teaching Tools
from the Lawrence Hall of Science.

Nerd Kards™
Photo Courtesy of

NERD KARDS

(Names Earning Respect & Dignity)
P O Box 900, Monroe, CT
06468-0900   203-925-9773
Fax   203-925-9773   Email
n e r d k a r d s @ s n e t . n e t
http://www.nerdkards.com (High
School to Adult)
This set of 102 Kards features scientists
with their major discoveries and
inventions. $ 13.45 per set.

PENTON OVERSEAS, INC.
Contact Hugh Penton, Sr.   2470
Impala Dr, Carlsbad, CA 92008
800-748-5804 760-431-0060, ext 681
Fax 760-431-8110
Email penton@cts.com
http://www.pentonoverseas.com
Distributor (Elementary School)
Ask for brochure.   Science Series by
Twin Sister Productions: I'd Like to
Be A..:   Astronaut, Paleontologist,
Entomologist,   Marine   Biologist,
Chemist, Zoologist, Meteorologist,
Physicist. Each title includes an audio

**I'd Like to Be an Entomologist
Audiocassette & Activity Book**
Photo Courtesy of Penton Overseas

cassette, 24-page lyric activity book, coloring pages, and brain-buster fact
sheets for enrichment learning.

PHYSICS OF TOYS DEMONSTRATION SET # 71938-02 $ 165.00 PHYSICS FUN AND DEMONSTRATIONS MANUAL # 58225 $ 13.50
CENCO, 3300 Cenco Parkway, Franklin Park, IL 60131-1364
800-262-3626 Fax 800-814-0607 http://www.cenconet.com Retail
(All ages)
This set of 23 familiar toys demonstrate physical principles as explained
in the accompanying manual.

PITSCO
1002 E Adams, P O Box 1708, Pittsburg, KS 66762-1708
800-835-0686 800-358-4983 http://www.pitsco.com
Fax 800-533-8104 Manufacturer Distributor Retail Mail Order
(Elementary School to College)
Ask for 432-page catalog. Major distributor of science materials,
including books, new science toys, video, and more. Over 600 new
products.

SCIENCE & NATURE DISTRIBUTORS
A division of Downeast Concepts, Inc., 20 Downeast Drive,
Yarmouth, ME 04096 800-344-5555 Fax 800-457-7087 Customer
Service 888-273-0946 Distributor Wholesale (Elementary School)
Ask for 88-page catalog. Large variety of science toys, games, books,
and lab equipment. Product categories include space & flight, earth
science, life science, physical science, science kits, brain games,
novelties, books, posters, and lab equipment.

SOMERVILLE HOUSE
3080 Yonge St, Suite 5000, Toronto, Ontario, Canada M4N 3N1
800-387-9776 Fax 800-260-9777 416-488-5938 Fax 416-488-5506
Email sombooks@goodmedia.com   http://www.sombooks.com
Manufacturer Distributor Wholesale (Elementary School)
Ask for 32-page catalog. The Bones Book with plastic skeleton, dinosaur books with plastic skeletons, The Environmental Detective Kit. Books packaged with toy models. Also The Bug Book & Bottle, The Ultimate Science Kit, Snail Tongues and Spider Fangs, Bug Eyes and Butterfly Wings, Coral Reef, Birds of Prey, Insects and Spiders, Snakes and Lizards, and more.

TEACHER CREATED MATERIALS, INC.
Contact Steve Mitchell 6421 Industry Way, Westminster, CA 92683
714-891-2273 Fax 714-892-0283 Email alacola@teachercreated.com
http://www.teachercreated.com Manufacturer Wholesale Retail
Mail Order (Elementary School)
Ask for catalogs: Teacher Created Materials, Techworks, Curriculum Catalog, and Professional Developmental Seminars. Their goal is to help teachers keep up with new educational trends. Thematic Teaching Resources includes Weather, Human Body, Space/Solar System, and Ancient Civilizations. Techworks helps teachers use whatever hardware and software they have to teach the existing curriculum more effectively.

Chapter

3 | Construction Toys & Models

A G INDUSTRIES
Contact Aaron Tibbs   15335 N E 95th St, Redmond, WA 98052
800-233-7174 425-885-4599 Fax 425-885-4672
Email atibbs@whitewings.com   http://www.whitewings.com
Manufacturer Retail and Wholesale
(Elementary School to High School)
Ask for 12-page catalog. Educational kits for constructing paper airplane gliders, boats and origami. Whitewings series includes the History of Passenger Planes, Future of Flight, History of Jet Fighters, Racers, Space Shuttle, Science of Flight. Display cases for home and retail stores.

ACTION PRODUCTS INT'L, INC.
344 Cypress Road, Ocala, FL 34472 800-772-2846 352-687-2202
Fax 352-687-4961 Email sales@apii.com http://www.apii.com
Manufacturer Distributor Wholesale (Elementary School)
Educational toys about science, Woodkits (Prehistoric and Animals from nature), Space Replicas, Imagninetics, Science in Action, and much more.

CHAOS
10920 Schuetz Road, Suite 1, St. Louis, MO 63146-5799
888-944-0129 314-567-9097
Fax 314-567-9123
Manufacturer Retail Mail Order (Elementary School to High School)
Ask for brochure. Chaos, World of Motion, is a construction toy where an elevated marble falls though endless possible energy conversions created by the child or student. Award winning toy.

Chaos™
Photo Courtesy of Chaos

Tensegritoy
Photo Courtesy of Design Science Toys

DESIGN SCIENCE TOYS LTD.
Contact Don Rimsky 1362 Route 9, Tivoli, NY 12583 800-227-2316 914-756-4221 Fax 914-756-4223 Manufacturer Distributor Retail (Preschool to Adult)
Ask for 10-page catalog. Wooden puzzles: Pyrra, Soma, Rhoma, Vexa, Magna, Cube Octa, Quadrhom, Tetra, Dodeca. Puzzles and games: Chung Toi, Smile Tiles-Bananas. Manipulatives: Heaven's orb, Heaven's Pendant, Rhomblocks, Feebee, Wacbee, Turnabout, Rhomtop. Construction toys: Tensegritoy, Stik-Trix, Roger's Connection, Zometool. Projects: Globe Project, Octabug, and Synergy Ball.

Inventa System
Photo Courtesy of
Dimensions in Learning

DIMENSIONS IN LEARNING, INC.
P O Box 639, Forest Park, IL 60130 888-366-6628 708-366-6117 Fax 708-366-8348 Email nkokat@sprintmail.com Distributor (Elementary School to High School)
Ask for 24-page catalog. Distributor of Valiant Technology Ltd. educational materials from Great Britain. Products include Roamer, robot that teaches mathematics; Inventa, system of invention and design; Tronix, system of science and technology using electronics; and more.

DOWLING MAGNETS

Contact JoAnn Chew   P O Box 1829, Sonoma, CA 95476
800-624-6381 707-935-0352 Fax 707-935-1231
Email dowling@DowlingMagnets.com Manufacturer   Wholesale
(High School to Adult)
Magnets and magnetic materials of numerous shapes and dimensions for
educational use. Ask for catalog.

ELENCO ELECTRONICS

150 W Carpenter, Wheeling, IL 60090 800-533-2441 847-541-3800
Fax 847-520-0085 Email elenco@elenco.com http://www.elenco.com
Manufacturer Retail Mail Order (Middle School to Adult)
Ask for catalog and brochure on Elenco Electronics Kits. Kits are
designed for educational learning experiences for students and hobbyists.
Many, but not all, of these kits require soldering.

ELWOOD TURNER CO.

HC39 Box 132, Morrisville, VT
05661 802-888-3375
Fax 802-888-3155
Email turnertoys@aol.com
http://www.turnertoys.com
Manufacturer   Distributor
Wholesale   Retail Mail Order
(Preschool)
Ask for catalog. Manufacturer of
Quarks Creative Building System:
Building Toy for 3-Year-Olds. This toy
is also found on the desks of architects,
artists, and engineers. Innovative
wooden toys since 1979.

Quarks™
Photo Courtesy of Elwood Turner

**fischertechnik®
Construction Set**
Photo Courtesy of Fischertechnik

FISCHERTECHNIK

2420 Van Layden Way, Modesto, CA 9 5 3 5 6 E m a i l fischertechnik@t-online.de http://www.fischertechnik.de Distributor of Fischertechnik (Elementary School to High School) Ask for brochure. German manufactured construction sets, including Harbor Cranes, Industry Robots, IR Control Set, and many more. Manufacturer of construction toys for over 50 years.

Googoplex® Model
Photo Courtesy of
Googolplex Toy Systems

GOOGOLPLEX TOY SYSTEMS INC.

195A Royal Crest Court, Markham, Ontario L3R 9X6 Canada 905-479-0064 905-447-0506 Fax 905-477-8891 Manufacturer Wholesale Ask for brochure. The Googolplex Toy System is an educational construction system than can be used to teach a wide variety of scientific topics.

HOMECRAFTERS MANUFACTURING

1859 Kenion Point, Snellville, GA 30078 770-985-5460
Fax 770-978-3012 Email hmctoys@aol.com
http://homecrafters-mfg.com Manufacturer Wholesale and Retail
(Elementary School)
Ask for brochure describing "I Made My...Periscope!" kit and "I Made
My...Kaleidoscope!" kit and other Home Crafted Toys.

K'NEX INDUSTRIES, INC.

Education Division, 2990 Bergey
Road, P O Box 700, Hatfield, PA
19440 800-543-5639 215-997-7722
Fax 215-996-4222
Email knex@provicenet.com
http://www.knex.com Manufacturer
(Elementary School to High School)
A unique, educational construction toy.
Science educational products include
Classroom Super Set & Educator
Guide, Solar System Set, Simple
Machines Sets.

**K'nex® Hyperspace
Training Tower**
Photo Courtesy of K'nex Industries

**Lego® System
Celestial Stinger**
Photo Courtesy of Lego Dacta

LEGO DACTA - THE EDUCATIONAL DIVISION OF LEGO SYSTEMS, INC.

555 Taylor Rd, P. O. Box 1600, Enfield, CN 06083-1600 800-527-8339 Manufacturer Retail and Wholesale Distributed by PITSCO 800-362-4308 (Elementary School to High School)

Gear, lever and pulley toys, Technic classroom kits, Technic control centers, teacher's guide books, Pneumatics, Logowriter Robotics for Apple and MS-DOS, Control Lab for Apple and MS-DOS.

LASY® Didact
Photo Courtesy of MaST Distribution

MAST DISTRIBUTION INC.

Distributor of LASY Toys, 54 Ballymore Drive, Aurora, Ontario L4G 7E6, Canada 888-553-6278 905-727-2985 Fax 905-727-3933 Email dnniesin@netrover.com http://www.lasy.com Distributor Wholesale (Elementary School)

Ask for 24-page LASY Didact (Educational) catalog. LASY is a quality, Made-in-Germany, construction toy. Many educational, scientific, and technology-oriented toys are available.

MAYFLOWER DEVELOPMENT AND TRADING CORP.

P O Box 705, Bellevue, WA 98009 425-747-7766 Fax 425-957-9384 Email switchon@concentric.net http://www.concentric.net/~switchon Manufacturer Wholesale Retail Mail Order (Elementary School to High School)

Manufacturer of Switch On!: Innovative Electronic Building Blocks. Have fun setting up easy-to-connect, safe circuit blocks to switch on: a light bulb, a fire engine, a flashing door bell, an electric fan, or create your own circuit. An excellent, fun way to teach electrical circuits to children.

MIDWEST MODEL SUPPLY CO.

12040 S Aero Dr, Plainfield, IL 60544 800-573-7029 815-254-2151 Fax 815-254-2445 Email mwmodelsup@aol.com Distributor Wholesale Quantity School Orders.

Ask for literature. Source for Estes Rockets & accessories, bridge building kits, aero-space models, plane programs, mousetrap racers, and model making materials.

MIDWEST PRODUCTS CO., INC.

400 S Indiana St, P. O. Box 564, Hobart, IN 46342 800-348-3497 219-942-1134 Fax 219-942-5703 Email tom@midwestproducts.com http://www.midwestproducts.com Retail Mail Order (Elementary School to High School)

Ask for 15-page catalog. Source of materials for model aviation, model bridge building, and kites.

Mouse Trap Racing Kit
Photo Courtesy of Midwest Products

OWI INCORPORATED

Contact Craig Morioka   1160 Mahalo Place, Compton, CA
90220-5443 310-638-4732 Fax 310-638-8347
Email owi@ix.netcom.com   http://www.owirobot.com
Manufacturer Wholesale (Nine Years to Adult)
Ask for brochure on Robotics and for information on retail distributors.
This manufacturer makes several different robotic kits requiring different
levels of assembly sophistication. The new Triple Action Solar Car Kit
allows batteries or solar power with a multi-speed transmission.

PARALLEL UNIVERSE CORPORATION

2201 Deschenes St, Ottawa, Ontario, Canada   K2B 6N2
888-877-5556 613-761-7658 Fax 613-722-4750
Email   parallel@magi.com   http://www.magi.com/~parallel
Manufacturer Distributor Wholesale Retail Mail Order
(Preschool to Elementary School)
Ask for brochure. This company designs print tissue paper patterns,
similar to dress patterns, that are traced over cardboard boxes to create
children's toys. Patterns include flying saucer, tug boat, castle, treasure
chest, and more.

PLAYWERKS, INC.

4405 Engle Road, Fort Wayne, IN 46804 800-598-7470 219-432-5328
Fax 219-432-5461 http://www.playwerkstoys.com Manufacturer
Wholesale (Elementary School)
Ask for brochure. Reusable stick-on figures activity sets with play board
include Space Station, Ocean Adventure, Dinosaurs, and more.

QUEST AEROSPACE
A division of Toy Biz, Inc. 350 East 18th St, Yuma, AZ 85364
800-858-7302 ext 110 Manufacturer Retail Mail Order
(High School)
Ask for 35-page catalog. Rockets and accessories for model rocketry.

R/C PRODUCTS
P O Box 127, Pleasanton, CA 94566 510-846-1767 Fax 510-846-1855
Email rockmck@pacbell.net http://www.wedgits.com Manufacturer
(Elementary School to Adult)
Wedgits is a construction toy of wedged shapes from an original cube.
It teaches spatial skills and is great creative fun. Ages 3 to 103.

RAMONA ENTERPRISES, INC.
80 Apparel Way, San Francisco, CA 94124 800-RAMONA-5
415-695-0200 Fax 415-695-0238 Manufacturer Wholesale
(Elementary School to Middle School)
Ask for brochure. Manufacturer of Gear-O-Matic, a toy that teaches how
gears change speeds, forces, and motions. Purchase on school letterhead.

SAFARI LTD.
Museum Quality Creative Toys, P O Box 630685, Miami, FL 33163
800-554-5414 305-621-1000 Fax 800-766-7841
http://www.safariltd.com Distributor Wholesale (All Ages)
129-page catalog is filled with quality science toys, including animal
replicas, activities, puzzles, science toys, woodcraft, games, and posters.

SUN-MATE CORP.

8223 Remmet Ave, Canoga Park, CA 91304   818-883-7766
Fax 818-883-8171   http://www.sun-mate.com   Manufacturer
Wholesale (Elementary School)
Science educational solar toys, wooden motor kits, adventure kits, and more.

TREE BLOCKS

Contact Terri Smith=Oppen 21103 Mulholland Dr, Woodland Hills,
CA 91364 800-873-4960 818-992-4569 Fax 818-348-9639
Email   elves@treeblocks.com   http://www.treeblocks.com
Manufacturer (Preschool to Elementary School)
Tree Blocks are building blocks cut from smooth real tree branches.
Using these building blocks one feels the complexity of nature.

TREE OF KNOWLEDGE

Contact Henry Bunzl, Managing Director Yasur, D. N. Misgav
20150, Israel 972-4-9960320 Fax 972-4-9969244 Manufacturer
Distributor (Elementary School to High School)
Ask for brochure. Manufacturer of Scientific Experiment Kits.

VECTA BLOCKS INC.

Contact Scott Jones 1515 Pitfield, St. Laurent, Quebec, Canada H4S 1G3 514-956-9300 Email vecta@openface.ca Manufacturer (Elementary School to High School) Vecta blocks are unique building blocks manufactured with Aerospace technology. They can be used to construct very precise, three-dimensional geometric figures such as the Archimedian polyhedra and even more complex polyhedra. These blocks can build "Buckeyball" on

**Vecta Blocks®
Construction System**
Photo Courtesy of Vecta Blocks

several scales of size, also known as the carbon-60 molecule. They can also build regular structures such as geodesic domes, helicopters and unlimited creative structures.

W J FANTASY INC.

Contact John McGrath 955 Connecticut Ave, Bridgeport, CT 06607 800-222-7529 203-333-5212 Fax 203-366-3826 Distributor Wholesale (Elementary School)

Building blocks for young children including Mini Bug Blocks, Endangered Wild Life Blocks, and Farmyard Friends.

ZOMETOOL

**1526 South Pearl Street, Denver, CO   80210   888-966-3386
303-733-2880   Fax 303-733-3116   Email sales@zometool.com
http://www.zometool.com Manufacturer (Elementary School to
Adult)**
The Zome System is a versatile, creative construction toy used by
mathematicians, scientists, engineers and architects. Yet, it is perfect as
a classroom teaching tool as well as creative play. The various possible
construction angles reflect the forces of physics and nature. Teacher kits,
student kits, researcher kits, and lesson plans available.

Chapter

4

Games

ABJECT MODERNITY LTD.

916 St. James St., Winnipeg, Manitoba, Canada R3H 0K3 888-260-8465 204-543-4220   Fax 204-774-8231 http://www.thestone.net

Manufacturer (Elementary School to High School)

Manufacturer of The Stone. The Stone is a toy, necklace, and Internet based game. The cryptic symbols on each stone match only one other Stone. These symbols connect the owner with one other Stonemate and act as the password to the Web site. Although this toy is not classically scientific, it brings you into an unique Internet game.

**SET® Game of
Visual Perception**
Photo Courtesy of Absolute Fun

ABSOLUTE FUN - INTERGENERATIONAL TOYS AND GAMES

Contact Kathleen Evans 15446 E El Lago, Fountain Hills, AZ   85268 800-351-7765   602-837-8217   Fax 602-816-4961 Email K2E2@aol.com http://www.setgame.com Distributor Retail Mail Order   (Elementary School to Adult)

Ask for brochures.   Distributor of award winning games, including SET, the Family Game of Visual Perception. SET is available as a card game and as a computer game (PC or Mac).   Other games include Triology and Five Crowns.

Onto the Desert Game
Photo Courtesy of Ampersand Press

AMPERSAND PRESS

Contact Amy Mook   750 Lake St, Port Townsend, WA 98368 800-624-4263 360-379-5187 Fax 360-379-0324 Email   mooburg@olympus.net http://www.ampersandpress.com Manufacturer Wholesale Retail Mail Order (Elementary School to Adult)

Ask for brochure. Manufacturer of games, including The Garden Game, The Bug Game, Onto the Desert Game, Predator Game, The Hummingbird Game, AC/DC Game, Into the Forest Game, Good Heavens! comet game, Oh Wilderness game, and Krill, a game about whales.

ARISTOPLAY

Contact Steve Nelson 450 S Wagner Rd, Ann Arbor, MI   48103
800-634-7738 734-995-4353
Fax 734-995-4611
Email   SNelson@aristoplay.com
http://www.aristoplay.com
Manufacturer   Retail Mail Order (Elementary School to Adult)
Ask for 32-page catalog, Games with an Aptitude. These board games that make learning fun include Animal Families, Don't Bug Me, NOVA True Science, SomeBody about anatomy, Constellation Station, Dinosaurs & Things, MARS 2020, and many more.

MARS 2020™ Game
Photo Courtesy of Aristoplay

BINARY ARTS CORP.

Contact Jennifer Koshute 1321 Cameron St, Alexandria, VA 22314
800-468-1864 703-549-4999 Fax 703-549-6210
Email jkoschute@puzzles.com http://www.puzzles.com
Manufacturer Distributor Wholesale (Elementary School to Adult)
Ask for 20-page catalog. Award winning games and puzzles include Rush Hour 2, Visual Brainstorms, Port to Port, Block by Block, Brick by Brick, Back-Spin, Top-Spin, Switch Back, Spin-Out, Nature's Spaces, Izzi, and many more.

CHANNEL CRAFT & DIST. INC.

P O Box 101, North Charleroi, PA 15022 800-232-4FUN 412-489-4900 Fax 412-489-0773 http://www.channelcraft.com Manufacturer Distributor Wholesale (Elementary School to Adult) Ask for 35-page catalog. Quality wooden toys, puzzles, and games made in USA, including Yo-Yo's, Jacob's Ladder, Boomerangs, Tops, Brain Teaser, Mind Bogglers, and more.

CHILD'S PLAY

Contact Joe Gardner   67 Minot Ave, Auburn, ME   04210 800-472-0099 Fax 800-854-6989 973-731-3777 Fax 973-731-3740 cplay@mail.idt.net Manufacturer (Preschool to Elementary School) Ask for 24-page catalog. Books, toys and games include Time Tunnel, Bats, Spiders, Children of the Sun (Astronomy), Metamorphoscs (Butterflies and Frogs), Sorting and Matching, Shape and Color, Arithmetic Games, and more.

Sound Bytes™
Photo Courtesy of
Eberhard, Von Huene & Associates

EBERHARD, VON HUENE & ASSOCIATES

346, rue Aime Vincent, Vaudreuil, Quebec, Canada J7V 5V5 514-424-0186 Fax 514-455-5126 Email eberhard@globale.net Manufacturer (Elementary School to Adult) Ask for brochure. Manufacturer of Sound Bytes, the verbal game in which a player's recorded verbal statements are "sliced 'n diced" when replayed so that the information can be recovered and understood by another player. Fun potential for classroom science games.

EDUCATIONAL INSIGHTS

Contact Customer Service Department 16941 Keegan Ave, Carson, CA 90746 800-995-4436 310-884-2000 Fax 800-995-0506 Email service@edin.com http://www.edin.com Manufacturer Retail and Wholesale (Elementary School)

Ask for 32-page catalog. GeoSafari computer games, Mini-Museums, Mystery Rock, Exploring Ecology, Natural Collections, Mysteries of Light, Mysteries of Magnetism, Adventures in Science series has 12 different projects, Science Safari Stickers, Fantastic Cards on science subjects, Animal Big Books 14" x 20", Bug Viewers, Dino Checkers, Dino Tic Tac Toe.

ENGINUITY LLC

P O Box 20607, San Jose, CA 95160 888-618-4263 Fax 408-268-9740 Email andy@enginuity.com http://www.enginuity.com Manufacturer Wholesale Retail Mail Order (Elementary School to Adult) Manufacturer of educational games, Stack 21, Tilez!, Doubles Wild, Target, and Diangle! Games teach spatial relations, addition, memory skills, and graphic skills.

Tilez!™
Color Matching Game
Photo Courtesy of Enginuity

Endangered
A Game about Animals
Photo Courtesy of Family Games

FAMILY GAMES INC.
P O Box 97, Snowdon, Montreal, Canada   H3X-3T3   800-291-1176
514-485-1834   Fax   514-485-2944
Manufacturer   Wholesale
(Elementary School)
Ask for 18-page catalog. Educational games, puzzles, and activities. Science products include MoonDust (paint natures creatures with colored powder), Too Cool Kit Mad Scientist Party, Tantrix award-winning puzzles and games, and more.

MOONSHOT The Game™
Photo Courtesy of The Galactic Attic

THE GALACTIC ATTIC
1102 Dartmouth St, Chattanooga, TN   37405   888-240-4415
423-756-0306   Fax   423-756-2237
Email galactic@voy.net
http://www.galacticattic.com
Manufacturer   Retail Mail Order
(Elementary School to Adult)
Ask for brochure. Manufacturer of board game, MOONSHOT, that chronicles the epic adventure of America's historic first leaps into space. Ages 10 years to adult. Designed for the collector; limited first edition.

GARY AND RIEDEL CO., INC.

265 Benton Stree, Stratford, CT
06497 800-255-8697
Fax 203-380-5299
http://www.all-toys.com
Manufacturer   Distributor
Wholesale (Elementary School to
High School)

Star Hop Game
Photo Courtesy of Gary and Riedel Co.

Ask for brochure. Manufacturer of
teaching games, including Krypto,
Fraction Krypto, Primary Krypto,
Sum-Words, Circulation, Space Hop,
Star Hop, Molecule Maker, and
Endangered Species.

KADON ENTERPRISES, INC.

Contact Kate Jones 1227 Lorene Dr, Suite 16, Pasadena, MD 21122
410-437-2163 Email kadon@gamepuzzles.com
http://www.gamepuzzles.com Manufacturer Retail (Elementary
School to Adult)
Ask for 15-page catalog of Gamepuzzles: for the Joy of Thinking. This
company specializes in sophisticated games and puzzles for the creative
thinker.

KOLBE CONCEPTS, INC.

P O Box 15667, Phoenix, AZ 85060 602-840-9770 Fax 602-952-2706
http://www.kolbe.com Manufacturer Retail (All ages)
Ask for brochure. Think-ercises, Glop Shop - inventor's assortment, Go
Power - science experiments, Using Your Senses, Solar Power Winners
- experiment book, Decide & Design - inventor's book.

KOPLOW GAMES, INC.

369 Congress St, Boston, MA 02210 800-899-0711 617-482-4011 Fax 617-482-3423 Manufacturer (Elementary School to Adult)
Ask for 28-page catalog. Manufacturer of dice and dice games, including numbered dice of all shapes for math and science. Action Fractions is an activity for teaching fractions ages 7 and up. Sand timers, pawns, bells, chips, stickers, rubber dice, glow-in-the-dark dice, and glass stones.

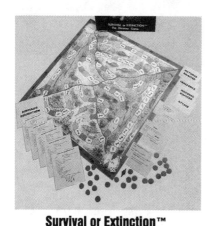

Survival or Extinction™
The Dinosaur Game
Photo Courtesy of Latz Chance Games

LATZ CHANCE GAMES, INC.

P O Box 72308, Marietta, GA 30007-2308   888-524-4263
770-579-6173   Fax 770-565-2756
Manufacturer   Wholesale
(Elementary School to Adult)
Ask for brochures. Science games include the award winning dinosaur game, Survival or Extinction, as well as Dinosaurs Across the Curriculum, Dinocardz, and Science Series Rock 'n Learn.

THE LIVING & LEARNING CO.

1632 Curtis Street, Berkeley, CA 94702 800-306-3013 Fax 510-527-9212
Orders: 4383 Hecktown Rd, Ste GA-1, Bethlehem, PA 10820 800-521-3218   Fax 800-582-8268   Manufacturer   Wholesale (Preschool to Elementary School)
Ask for 14-page Science Pre-School Puzzles catalog. Products also include Jam Jar Science-Bugs (Bug collecting), Where in the Wild? (Game), Explore! (Game), and many more.

MINDWARE

2720 Patton Rd, Roseville, MN
55113-1138 800-999-0398
Fax 888-299-9273 Retail Mail Order
(All Ages)
Ask for 40-page catalog. Products
include many science toys, puzzles,
and games.

Planet Earth
Earth Science Kit
Photo Courtesy of Mindware

PROFESSOR SMARTY GAMES,INC.

P O Box 2043, Davidson, NC 28036
800-763-6722   Fax 704-331-7598
http://www.professorsmarty.com
Manufacturer
(Elementary School to High School)
Manufacturer of games, including Bug
World, Predators & Prey, and Sharks.

Predators & Prey Game
Photo Courtesy of
Professor Smarty Games

SAFARI LTD.

Museum Quality Creative Toys, P O Box 630685, Miami, FL 33163
800-554-5414   305-621-1000   Fax   800-766-7841
http://www.safariltd.com Distributor Wholesale (All Ages)
129-page catalog is filled with quality science toys, including animal
replicas, activities, puzzles, science toys, woodcraft, games, and posters.

SCIENCE & NATURE DISTRIBUTORS

A division of Downeast Concepts, Inc., 20 Downeast Drive,
Yarmouth, ME 04096 800-344-5555 Fax 800-457-7087 Customer
Service 888-273-0946 Distributor Wholesale (Elementary School)
Ask for 88-page catalog. Large variety of science toys, games, books,
and lab equipment. Product categories include space & flight, earth
science, life science, physical science, science kits, brain games,
novelties, books, posters, and lab equipment.

SENTOSPHERE USA

81 E Second St, New York, NY 10003 212-674-8202
Fax 212-505-9526 Manufacturer Wholesale (Elementary School)
Ask for brochure. Products include Follow Your Nose (a game with 30
distinct aroma samples), Perfume Maker (chemically create more than
100 different fragrances), and many preschool wood puzzles of nature
and science.

SMETHPORT SPECIALTY CO.

One Magnetic Avenue, Smethport, PA 16749 800-772-8697 814-887-5508   Fax 814-887-9272 Manufacturer   Wholesale (Elementary School)
Ask for 32-page catalog. Science magnetic play sets, where magnetic characters are placed on a scenic board, include Magnetic Dinosaurs, Ocean Adventure, Magnetic Zoo, and Magnetic Adventure.   Many other products include educational games and puzzles.

Magnet Playboard Set
Photo Courtesy of Smethport Specialty

TEDCO, INC.

Contact Jane Shadle 498 S Washington St, Hagerstown, IN 47346
800-654-6357 765-486-4527 Fax 765-489-5752
Email jane@tedcotoys.com   http://www.tedcotoys.com
Manufacturer Distributor (Elementary School to Adult)
Ask for 10-page catalog. Toys include the TEDCO Gyroscope, games & mazes, The Original Blocks and Marbles, Explorer Wrist Compass, Magna-Trix, Rattleback, Right Angle Prisms, Solar Science Kit, and more.

TRIGRAM S. A.

8a puits-godet, CH-2000 Neuchatel, Switzerland 41-32-721-28-38
Fax 41-32-721-28-46 Email info@trigam.ch http://www.trigam.ch
Manufacturer Wholesale (All Ages)
Ask for brochure. 3-D puzzles and games based on mathematical theories. Products include Pentagor, Trigam Circus, Trigam 2, Zodiacube, DRHOMBX, Magic Diamond, Geometric Pearls, Twin Golden Diamond, and Trigam X.

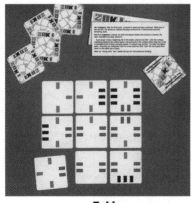

Zoki
Mentally Challenging Games
Photo Courtesy of
Zoki Game Company

ZOKI GAME COMPANY

15445 Ventura Blvd, Suite 79,
Sherman Oaks, CA 91403
888-616-1987 310-260-1019
Fax 310-451-0014
http://www.zoki.com Manufacturer
(All Ages)
Manufacturer of Zoki, set of small tiles with different colored numbers for playing numerous educational games using classifying and thinking skills.

Chapter

5

Nature Toys

BEAR CREEK TOYS, INC.

P O Box 247, Woodinville, WA 98072 800-232-7275 425-788-8104 Fax 425-844-2262 **Manufacturer Wholesale (Elementary School)**

Ask for 8-page catalog. Science and Nature Products include Critter Catcher Gift Set, Nature Net, Activity Jar, Bones & Rocks Earth Science Kit, Treasure Adventure, Plant Patch Growing Kits, Plant Patch Shovel, and more.

Young Naturalist Activity Jar
Photo Courtesy of Bear Creek Toys

BULLYLAND INC.
65 W 55th Street, 4th Floor, New York, NY 10019 212-974-9815 Fax
212-974-9814 Email bully@bullyland.de http://www.bullyland.de
Manufacturer Distributor Wholesale (Elementary School)
Replicas of prehistoric people, animals, dinosaurs, insects.
Glow-in-the-Dark Skeletons, and more.

CALIFORNIA PACIFIC DESIGNS
P O Box 2660, Alameda, CA 94501 510-521-7914 Fax 510-865-0851
Manufacturer Wholesale (Elementary School)
Ask for brochures. Manufacturer of stickers and craft kits about animals
from nature: Earthwing Collector Stickers, Tin & Craft Kits, Mini Wood
Craft Puzzles, and Glass Paperweights.

CASCADE TOY
P O Box 1425, North Bend, WA 98045 800-882-8087 206-888-4600
Fax 206-888-9699 Email cascadetoy@worldnet.att.net
http://www.cascadetoy.com Manufacturer Distributor Wholesale
(Elementary School)
Realistic wildlife stuffed animals.

CHILDCRAFT EDUCATION CORP.
20 Kilmer Road, P. O. Box 3081, Edison, NJ 08818-3081
800-631-5652 http://childcraft.com Distributor Retail
(Preschool to Elementary School)
Ask for the 200-page catalog. Math toys, aquariums, plant growing kit,
seashells, root garden, ant farm, microscope, optical toys, magnetic toys,
weather materials, globes. Educational materials.

CHILDWOOD

Contact Karen Beierle 8873 Woodbank Dr, Bainbridge Island, WA 98110 800-362-9825 206-842-9290 Fax 206-842-5107 Email childwood@aol.com Manufacturer   Retail Mail Order (Preschool and Elementary School)

Ask for 14-page catalog. Six science themes are packaged with sturdy, full-color, wooden magnetic figures. All hands-on science sets include stories, activities and reproducible mini-books. Sets include Life Cycles: The Butterfly, The Hen and The Frog; The Farm; Sealife; The Bear Cave; Dinosaurs; and Weather.

CLUB EARTH

A division of Easy Aces, Inc. 30 Martin St, Suite 381, Cumberland, RI 02864 800-327-8415   401-333-3090   Fax 401-333-3123 Distributor Wholesale (All Ages)

Ask for brochure. Toys, puppets, and novelties related to animals and living creatures of the Earth.

CURIOUS DISCOVERIES, INC.

7911 Windspray Drive, Summerfield, NC 27358 800-585-2386 910-643-0432   Fax 910-643-0438   http://www.curiouskids.com Manufacturer Wholesale (Elementary School)

Science discovery kits, nature products, animal replicas, and much more.

DAMERT COMPANY

1609 4th Street, Berkeley, CA 94710 800-231-3722 510-524-7400
Fax 510-524-4466 Email damert@aol.com http://www.damert.com
Manufacturer Wholesale (Elementary School to Adult)
Ask for 36-page catalog. Science toys include 3-D Slide Puzzles, Jungle Bungles puzzles, Concentra puzzle, Tiazzle Puzzles, Master Triazzles, coffee mugs, bulletin boards, many science mobiles, StarShines astronomy stickers, diffraction toys, Laser Top, Spiral Mobiles, Turbo Sparkler YoYo, liquid crystal toys and novelties, Little Critter Kaleidoscope, Butterflies of the World, bird feeder kit, Zoetrope, Vector Flexor, Echo Rocket, Spacephones, Tornado Tube, science charts and posters.

I Dig Dinosaurs™
Photo Courtesy of Earth Lore

EARTH LORE LTD.

94 Durand Road, Winnipeg, MB R2J
3T2, Canada 800-440-2630
204-654-1030   Fax 204-654-1018
http://www.earthlore.mb.ca
Manufacturer   Wholesale
(Elementary School)
Ask for brochure. Manufacturer of I Dig Dinosaurs, excavation kits where dinosaur models are hidden in a sand enclosure.

EDMUND SCIENTIFIC COMPANY

101 E Gloucester Pike, Barrington, NJ 08007-1380 800-728-6999 609-573-3488 Fax 609-573-6272 http://www.edsci.com Retail (All ages)

Ask for 112-page science reference catalog for educators. Since 1942 this well known scientific optical supplier also sells many other items including lasers, microscopes, camera/monitor systems, science classroom anatomy models, nature kits, laboratory safety equipment, balances, weather instruments, timers, magnets, small motors & pumps, robot kits, earth science kits, telescopes, museum animal replicas, and unique classroom materials for teachers.

EDUCATIONAL INSIGHTS

Contact Customer Service Department 16941 Keegan Ave, Carson, CA 90746 800-995-4436 310-884-2000 Fax 800-995-0506 Email service@edin.com http://www.edin.com Manufacturer Retail and Wholesale (Elementary School)

Ask for 32-page catalog. GeoSafari computer games, Mini-Museums, Mystery Rock, Exploring Ecology, Natural Collections, Mysteries of Light, Mysteries of Magnetism, Adventures in Science series has 12 different projects, Science Safari Stickers, Fantastic Cards on science subjects, Animal Big Books 14" x 20", Bug Viewers, Dino Checkers, Dino Tic Tac Toe.

ENVIRO-MENTAL TOY CO. INC.

P O Box 580186, Flushing, NY 11358 718-428-8972 Manufacturer Distributor Wholesale (All Ages)

Ask for brochure. Products include Sun-Sational Science Tee Shirts with natural science animal pictures that are black & white indoors, but instantly change to full color when exposed to sunshine. Indoors they fade back to black & white.

EXPLORATOY

19560 S Rancho Way, Dominguez Hills, CA 90220   310-884-3490
800-995-9290 http://www.exploratoy.com Manufacturer Wholesale
(Elementary School)
Ten-page catalog.   Beakman's World Inquizator computerized quiz
machine, Early Start learning machine, Critter Carnival insect house,
Creature Catcher, The Antworks, Bug Pals, Riddle Rocks, Explorascope
microscope, Test Tube Science in six science packs, Cosmic Observing
Station telescope, Star Tower toy planetarium.

FELDSTEIN & ASSOCIATES INC.

1946 N 13th St, Toledo, OH 43624   419-242-6500   Fax 419-242-5939
Distributor Wholesale (Elementary School)
Ask for brochure. Distributor of The Singing Bird Book with 12 of the
most recognized bird songs at the touch of a button.

Folkmanis® Puppets
Photo Courtesy of Folkmanis

FOLKMANIS, INC.

1219 Park Avenue, Emeryville, CA
94608 510-658-7677
Fax 510-654-7756
http://www.folkmanis.com
Manufacturer Wholesale
(Elementary School)
Folkmanis Puppets are quality life-like
reproductions of natures creatures.
Numerous variety from bears to
butterflies.

FRANCIS FAMILY TOYS LTD.
1314 Rufina Circle #A9, Santa Fe, NM 87505 505-473-4501
Fax 505-473-4519 Manufacturer Wholesale (Elementary School)
Ask for brochure. Manufacturer of CREATEures, stuffed cotton animals that you paint. Also, heirloom quality folk toys including Jacob's Ladder, Tie Dye Kit, and preschool wooden toys.

GEOCENTRAL
Contact Cindy Vader 1721 Action Ave, Napa, CA 94559 800-231-6083 707-224-7500   Fax 707-224-7400 Email cindy@geocentral.com Manufacturer Wholesale (Elementary School to High School)
Quantity sets of rocks and minerals for retail sale. Flat boxes of mineral and fossil assortments.   Sea shell glow night lights. Agate bookends. Twenty four-page catalog.

Fossils, Minerals & Seashells
Photo Courtesy of Geocentral

Root-Vue-Farm™
Photo Courtesy of Horticultural Sales

HORTICULTURAL SALES PRODUCTS
505C Grand Caribe Isle, Coronado, CA 92118 888-ROOTVUE
619-423-9399 Fax 619-423-9398
Email rootvue@aol.com
http://members.aol.com/rootvue
Manufacturer (Elementary School to High School)
Manufacturer of Root-Vue-Farm: Watch carrots, radishes and onions take form underground through a glass window. Other products include Worm-Vue Wonders, Wonderfinders, Powersphere, and Naturestation.

I.G.C. GIOCATTOLI MAX SAS
Zona Instriale 43, Lanchiano, C H, Italy 0872-42205 Fax 0872-43281
Manufacturer Wholesale (Elementary School to High School)
Ask for 44-page catalog. Quality microscope kits, microscope monitors, gardening kits, chemistry sets, and telescopes.

IDEAL SCHOOL SUPPLY COMPANY
11000 S Lavergne Ave, Oak Lawn, IL 60453 800-845-8149
http://www.ifair.com Distributor Retail Mail Order (Preschool to Elementary School)
Ask for the 50-page teacher catalog. Science measurement materials, chemistry experiment beakers and test tubes, equilateral prisms, physics pulleys, thermometers, classroom science kits, magnetic toys, natural science materials.

INSECT LORE
P O Box 1535, Shafter, CA   93263
800-LIVE-BUG 805-746-6047
Fax 805-746-0334
Email insect@lightspeed.net
http://www.insectlore.com
**Manufacturer Wholesale Retail
Mail Order (Elementary School)**
Ask for 32-page catalog. Distributor of
many science kits and books on nature's
creatures,   including   ant   farms,
butterflies, insects, plants & trees,
science project ideas, frogs and
amphibians, and nature videos.

Butterfly Pavilion
Photo Courtesy of Insect Lore

K & M INTERNATIONAL
1955 Midway Drive, Twinsburg, OH
44087   800-800-9678 216-963-8678
Fax 216-425-3777   **Manufacturer
Wholesale (Elementary School to
Adult)**
Anatomically accurate stuffed and
molded animals creatures of nature.
Stuffed products include National
Geographic WildLife Ledgends, AZA
Animals, Maddalena Series, African
Animals, Rainforest Animals, Animals
of the World, North American

Rainforest Lemurs
Photo Courtesy of K & M International

Animals, Aquaic Animals, puppets, and more. Molded products include
containers of small, hand-held animal toys and numerous varieties of kits,
puzzles, stickers, and more.

KIPP BROTHERS, INC.
240-242 S Meridian St, P. O. Box 157, Indianapolis, IN 46206
800-428-1153 317-634-5507 Fax 800-832-5477 Fax 317-634-5518
http://www.kippbro.com Importers Retail and Wholesale (All Ages)

Ask for 224-page catalog. Established in 1880 this distributor specializes in inexpensive toys, novelties, carnival and party items for quantity, dozen purchases. Science items include dinosaur tattoos, animal sounds, musical toys, tops, magnetic wheels, rubber and foam balls, kaleidoscopes, bird gliders, solar radiometer, telescopes, boomerangs, magnetized marbles, flying toys, kazoos, magnifying glasses, museum quality dinosaurs, and many, many more.

KLUTZ
455 Portage Ave, Palo Alto, CA 94306-2213 800-558-8944
Fax 800-524-4075 650-424-0739 Manufacturer Retail Mail Order (Elementary School to High School)

Ask for the 46-page Klutz Catalogue. Really fun toys and novelties. Amazon Worms, Smartballs, Smartrings, The Explorabook - a kids science museum in a book, ExploraCenter, Backyard Weather Station kit, Mega-Magnet Set, Backyard Bird Book with bird caller, The Aerobie Orbiter, Rubber Stamp Bug Kit, Vinyl Vermin, Kids Gardening Guide, World Record Paper Airplane Kit, The Arrowcopter, Megaballoons, Bubble Book, Zoetrope, juggling materials.

KRISTAL EDUCATIONAL INC.
Distributed by Ira Cooper, Inc., P O Box 2137, Woodinville, WA
98072   206-720-6264   Fax 206-720-6317
http://www.mysteriousart.com   Distributor Wholesale
(Elementary School to High School)
Ask for 26-page catalog. Mineral crystal growing kits, including Space
Age Crystal Kits; Crystal Spheres, Pyramids & Jewelry; Crystal Caves;
Dab'a'Dino (Paintable stuffed dinosaurs); National Geographic Society's
Expedition Series; Gem Tree Kits; Archeology Kits; and more.

LEAPFROG
Contact Scott Masline 1250 45th St, Suite 150, Emeryville, CA
94608 800-701-532 510-595-2470 Fax 510-595-2478
Email scottm@leapfrogtoys.com   http://www.leapfrogtoys.com
Manufacturer Wholesale (Elementary School)
Ask for catalog. Science toys include National Geographic Really Wild
Animals, an interactive electronic talking toy, and Space Explorer
Shuttle, a toy that talks when cards are inserted, teaching hundreds of
facts about astronomy.

LIGHTRIX, INC.
2132 Adams Ave, San Leandro, CA   94577   800-850-4656
510-577-7800 Fax 415-244-9795 Email dlr@lightrix.com
http://www.lightrix.com Manufacturer Wholesale (Elementary
School to Adult)
Holographic toys and novelties. Products include bright holograms of
nature & science, holographic sunglasses, Spectrix Visors, Eccentrix
diffraction discs, science puzzles, dinosaurs, and more.

LITTLE KIDS, INC.

Contact Jim Engle 222 Richmond St, Suite 302, Providence, RI
02903   800-545-5437   401-454-7600   Fax 401-455-0630
Manufacturer (Elementary School)
Ask for catalog. Science related toys include many various
bubble-making toys and realistically styled plush animals that make
sounds from actual animals.

THE LIVING & LEARNING CO.

1632 Curtis Street, Berkeley, CA 94702 800-306-3013
Fax 510-527-9212   Orders: 4383 Hecktown Rd, Ste GA-1,
Bethlehem, PA 10820 800-521-3218 Fax 800-582-8268
Manufacturer Wholesale (Preschool to Elementary School)
Ask for 14-page Science Pre-School Puzzles catalog. Products also
include Jam Jar Science-Bugs (Bug collecting), Where in the Wild?
(Game), Explore! (Game), and many more.

MRS. GROSSMAN'S PAPER CO.

Contact Jeff Shaw   3810 Cypress Drive, Petaluma, CA 94954
800-457-4570 707-763-1700 Fax 707-763-7121
Email jshaw@mrsgrossmans.com http://www.mrsgrossmans.com
Manufacturer Wholesale (Elementary School)
Ask for 74-page catalog. Peel-off stickers, idea books, and kits include
topics on dinosaurs, nature, ocean life, and animals.

MUSEUM PRODUCTS

84 Route 27, Mystic, CT   06355   800-395-5400   203-538-6433
Distributor Retail Mail Order (Elementary School to High School)
Ask for 56-page catalog. Unique toys and educational products from
science and nature.

NATIONAL ENERGY FOUNDATION

Contact Gary Swan 5225 Wiley Post Way, Suite 170, Salt Lake City, UT 84116 801-539-1406 Fax 801-539-1451 Email info@nef1.org http://www.nef1.org (Elementary School to High School)
This nonprofit organization provides programs and materials to help promote an awareness of energy-related issues. Ask for 15-page catalog of publications and science kits. Materials include Out of the Rock, a mineral resource and mining education program for K-8 produced in conjunction with the U. S. Bureau of Mines.

NATURE'S TOYLAND

Subsidiary of Penn-Plax, Inc., 720 Stewart Ave, Garden City, NY 11530 516-222-1020 Manufacturer Wholesale
(Elementary School to Adult)
This manufacturer of pet care products makes educational kits, including Tweety-Your First Bird Cage Kit, Tom and Jerry Hamster/Gerbil Home, The Little Mermaid Goldfish Aquarium and Collection Tank, The Little Mermaid Hermit Crab World, Ninja Turtles Collection Play Tank, Tweety-My First Bird Watching Kit, Bugs Bunny Rabbit/Guinea Pig Cage and Small Animal Habitats for hamsters and gerbils. See your local pet care retail store.

Canned Critters
Photo Courtesy of Northern Gifts

NORTHERN GIFTS INC.

Contact Bob MacKerricher 250-H Street, P O Box 8110-882, Blaine, WA 98231 800-665-0808 604-299-5050 Fax 604-299-0808 Manufacturer Wholesale Retail Mail Order (Elementary School)
Ask for 16-page catalog. Manufacturer of Canned Critters, plush toys sealed in a can with a complete description of each animal as it appears in nature. Canned Critters include Canned Black Bear, Moose, Sea Turtle, Raccoon, Buffalo, Beaver, Wolf, Loon, Bald Eagle, Penguin, Owl, Bat, Armadillo, Alligator, and many more.

PAPPA GEPPETTO'S TOYS VICTORIA LTD.

P O Box 3567, Blaine, WA 98231-3567 800-667-5407 Fax 800-973-5678 250-382-9975 Email pappa@mail.islandnet.com Manufacturer (Toys for Baby as well as All Ages)
Manufacturer of Skwish Classic, mobile Tranquility V, Wooden Mini Dinosaurs, and Flex-Bugs.

PARADISE CREATIONS

21789 Town Place Dr, Boca Raton, FL 33433 Manufacturer Phil Seltzer, 11806 Gorham Ave #7, Los Angeles, CA 90049   310-207-4451 Fax 310-207-6320   Distributor (Elementary School to High School) Ask for brochure. Fully articulated human anatomy skeletons that easily snap together, including The Skull, 14-inch and 23-inch Skeletons, Male Skeleton, Female Skeleton, and Bones-Organs-Muscles. Also Seashell Collector Sets.

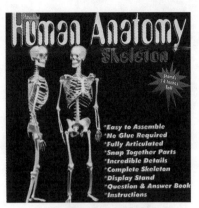

Human Anatomy Skeleton
Photo Courtesy of Paradise Creations

PIGMENT & HUE, INC.

Contact Howard Kurtz 8730-I Santa Monica Blvd, West Hollywood, CA 90069   800-850-8221   310-855-9581   Fax 310-855-9671 Manufacturer Wholesale (Elementary School)
Ask for 16-page catalog. Cards for kids to color combining art and science. They include place mats, posters, and Banners. Science products: Explore the Universe, Games at the Museum, Angelfish & Butterflyfish, Parrots, Tulips, Dinosaur Pals, Endangered Animals, and more.

PLAY VISIONS

1137 N 96th St, Seattle, WA 98103 Contact Mario DiPasquale 800-678-8697 Fax 206-524-2766 Email mariod@playvisions.com http://www.playvisions.com Manufacturer (Elementary School)
Ask for 50-page catalog. Telescopes, optical toys, Giant Rainforest Insects, reptiles & amphibians, Habitat nature model sets, dinosaur toy sets, vinyl Earth balls, Earth Squish Balls, Native American Arrowheads, and many inexpensive novelty items.

Banded Rock Rattlesnake
Photo Courtesy of Safari Ltd.

SAFARI LTD.
Museum Quality Creative Toys, P O
Box 630685, Miami, FL 33163
800-554-5414   305-621-1000
Fax 800-766-7841
http://www.safariltd.com
Distributor Wholesale (All Ages)
129-page catalog is filled with quality
science toys, including animal replicas,
activities,   puzzles,   science   toys,
woodcraft, games, and posters.

SCIENTIFIC EXPLORER, INC.
4020 E Madison, Suite 326, Seattle, WA   98112 800-900-1182
206-322-7611 Fax 206-322-7610 Email sciex@scientificexplorer.com
http://www.scientificexplorer.com   http://www.gettoys.com
Manufacturer Retail Mail Order (Elementary School to Adult)
Ask for 16-page catalog. Manufacturer of science and adventure kits
including Fun with Your Cat, Fun with Your Dog, Smithsonian
Adventures Series, Aerial Camera, High Altitude Launcher, Science of
Scent, Make Animal Soaps, Kitchen Science, Educational Cooking
Center, Nature Adventures, Exploring Electronics, Science of Sound, and
many more.

SMALL WORLD TOYS

5711 Buckingham Parkway, Culver City, CA 90230 800-421-4153
310-645-9680   Fax 310-410-9606   Manufacturer   Distributor
Wholesale (Preschool and Elementary School)
Gyroscopes, Gravity Graph, inflatable globes, Backyard Scientist, mineral
sets, Bug World, dinosaur skeleton kits, Polyopticon optical toy kits, Bug
Hotel, magnetic toys, Gigantic Glow Stars, dinosaur models, origami kits,
Whirlybirds, Newton's Yo-Yo, Finger Tops, Astronaut Food, animal sets,
magnifier toys, Sparkling Wheels, Relaxable Globe Balls.

SOMERVILLE HOUSE

3080 Yonge St, Suite 5000, Toronto, Ontario, Canada M4N 3N1
800-387-9776 Fax 800-260-9777 416-488-5938 Fax 416-488-5506
Email sombooks@goodmedia.com   http://www.sombooks.com
Manufacturer Distributor Wholesale (Elementary School)
Ask for 32-page catalog. The Bones Book with plastic skeleton, dinosaur
books with plastic skeletons, The Environmental Detective Kit. Books
packaged with toy models. Also The Bug Book & Bottle, The Ultimate
Science Kit, Snail Tongues and Spider Fangs, Bug Eyes and Butterfly
Wings, Coral Reef, Birds of Prey, Insects and Spiders, Snakes and
Lizards, and more.

TOY-RRIFIC, INC.

944 E 4th St, Los Angeles, CA 90013   888-869-7743
Fax 213-617-7502 Distributor Wholesale (Elementary School)
Ask for catalog. Science toys distributed include microscope, Wildlife
Study Set, and Super-Super Balls.

Instant Daphnia Kit
Photo Courtesy of Triops

TRIOPS, INC.
Educational Science Products,
P O Box 10852, Pensacola, FL 32524
800-200-3466 850-479-4415
Fax 850-479-3315 **Manufacturer**
Distributor Wholesale (Elementary
School to High School)
Ask for brochures and catalogs. Products include Instant Triops (eggs of this prehistoric creature hatch in water in 24 hours), Zooplankton, Instant Daphnia, Instant Killifish, Instant Green Algae, Instant Brine Shrimp, and more.

Tweber Nature Houses™
Photo Courtesy of TWC of America

TWC OF AMERICA, INC.
Contact Terry Weber 9663 Hwy 144 North, Kewaskum, WI 53040 800-301-7592 414-692-6835 Fax 414-692-6709 http://www.twcoa.com h t t p : / / w w w . t w e b e r . c o m Manufacturer Wholesale (Elementary School to Adult)
Ask for 8-page TWC Gifts Catalog, including quality products for nature lovers: Insect & Pond Nets, various wooden Nature Houses, bat houses, OBE II Bird Feeder, Colonial Birdhouse Kits. Ask for 8-page Tweber Backyard Explorer Gear Catalog, including products for the young nature lover: Play Tent, Nature Houses, Nature Exploring & Catch-All Nets, Leaf Press, Bird Houses, and Bird Feeders.

UNCLE MILTON INDUSTRIES, INC.

5717 Corsa Ave, Westlake Village, CA 91362-4001 800-869-7555
818-707-0800 Fax 818-707-0878 Email antfarm@ix.netcom.com
http://www.unclemilton.com Manufacturer Wholesale
(Elementary School)
Seven-page catalog contains Ant Farms (Milton Levine invented the Ant
Farm in 1956), Pocket Museums, Fossil Hunt, Krazy Klowns, Light-Up
Critter City, BugJug, Star Theater home planetarium, Super GeoScope
microscope, Hydro Greenhouse, Rock & Mineral Hunt, Surf Frogs. Surf
Frogs is a live frog habitat where frogs grow from tadpoles.

W J FANTASY INC.

Contact John McGrath 955
Connecticut Ave, Bridgeport, CT
06607 800-222-7529 203-333-5212
Fax 203-366-3826 Distributor
Wholesale (Elementary School)
Building blocks for young children
including Mini Bug Blocks,
Endangered Wild Life Blocks, and
Farmyard Friends.

**Endangered Wildlife
Building Blocks**
Photo Courtesy of W J Fantasy

WIT CRAFTS
**50 Main St, Malden, MA 02148 781-324-0114 Fax 781-322-7208
Email jqshan@aol.com Manufacturer Wholesale (All Ages)**
Ask for brochure. Hand-made, mahogany-wood novelty items that are both inspiring art and witty entertainment. Science items include Rolling Balls, Jigsaw Puzzles, Trees with Birds and Monkeys, Animals Set, Dinosaurs Set, Gears & Dial, and more.

Chapter

6

Novelties & Small Toys

ACCOUTREMENTS
P O Box 30811, Seattle, WA 98103   800-886-2221   425-349-3838
Fax 425-745-1743 http://www.accoutrements.com **Manufacturer**
Distributor Wholesale (Elementary School)
Carries numerous gifts and novelties, including Space Mucus, the
Computer Radio, the Brain Gelatin Mold, and much more.

AMERICAN PAPER OPTICS
Contact Andrew Balogh 3080 Bartlett Corporate Drive, Bartlett, TN
38133 800-767-8429   901-381-1515   Fax 901-381-1517
Email abalogh@lunaweb.net **Manufacturer Wholesale**
Retail Mail Order (Elementary School to Adult)
Manufacturer of Holiday Specs, paper eye glasses that create images
around small bright white holiday lights.

Brain Gelatin Mold
Photo Courtesy of Archie Mc Phee

ARCHIE MC PHEE
P. O. Box 30852, Seattle, WA 98103
206-745-0711   Fax   425-745-7143
Email   mcphee@mcphee.com
http://www.halcyon.com/mcphee/
Retail Mail Order   Retail store
located at 3510 Stone Way N, Seatle,
WA 206-545-8344 (All ages)
Ask for 15-page catalog.   Fun,
inexpensive toys and novelties. Insects,
bats, turtles, fish, dinosaurs, eye balls,
beanie with propeller, iguanas, wall
walker octopus.

BENJAMIN INTERNATIONAL
Contact Lynn Dimon   139 Bacon Pond, Woodbury, CT   06798
800-488-4699   Fax   888-488-4699   Email LDimon@aol.com
Manufacturer Distributor Wholesale (Elementary School to Adult)
Ask for 24-page catalog. Manufacturer and distributor of novelty items
including Glow-in-the-Dark Stars and Planets, Tornado Tube, Collectable
Tin Toy Animals, Sand Pets, LaserSpin, Hologram Glasses, Aero-Prop,
Hand Boiler, Drinking Bird, Kritterscopes, Lotus Puzzle, Blacklites,
Electronic Laser Ball, and Strobe Light.

CALIFORNIA PACIFIC DESIGNS

P O Box 2660, Alameda, CA 94501
510-521-7914   Fax 510-865-0851
Manufacturer   Wholesale
(Elementary School)
Ask for brochures. Manufacturer of
stickers and craft kits about animals
from nature: Earthwing Collector
Stickers, Tin & Craft Kits, Mini Wood
Craft Puzzles, and Glass Paperweights.

Dinosaur Stickers
Photo Courtesy of
California Pacific Designs

CARLISLE CO.

P O Box 21029, Carson City, NV 89721   800-233-3931
Fax 800-245-3306 Manufacturer Distributor Retail Mail Order
(Elementary School to Adult)
Ask for 24-page catalog. Novelties from science and nature including
Holographic Wands, Mobiles, Anti-Gravity Revolution, Lightning Balls,
Kinetic Chaos pendulum, Kinetic Sealife, Perpetual Motion Wheels,
Solar System motion space sculpture, Rave Wave dual-colored waves,
Spiral Timer, and much, much more.

CENTER ENTERPRISES, INC.

P O Box 331361, West Hartford, CT 06133-1361 800-542-2214
Fax 800-373-2923 http://www.centerenterprises.com
Manufacturer Wholesale (All Ages)
Ask for brochure. Manufacturer of rubber stamps for ink pads. Products
include Plane Geometry Stamps, Fraction Stamps, Animal Stamps,
Dinosaur Stamps, and many, many more sets of stamps.

**Wet 'n Wild
Squirting Handpuppets**
Photo Courtesy of Club Earth

CLUB EARTH

A division of Easy Aces, Inc. 30 Martin St, Suite 381, Cumberland, RI 02864 800-327-8415 401-333-3090 Fax 401-333-3123 **Distributor Wholesale (All Ages)** Ask for brochure. Toys, puppets, and novelties related to animals and living creatures of the Earth.

Computer Bug™
Photo Courtesy of
Computer Friendly Stuff

COMPUTER FRIENDLY STUFF, INC.

Contact William Martens 312 N May St, Suite 4A, Chicago, IL 60607 888-FUN-BUGS 312-491-0424 Fax 312-491-0136 Email wmartens@computerbug.com http://www.computerbug.com **Manufacturer Retail Mail Order (High School to Adult)** This computer screen saver, Monitor Morphs, is a face that comes on a CD-ROM and with movable arms that attach to the sides of a computer screen. A ten-inch plush computer bug, Computer Bug, is also available.

COPERNICUS

Contact Harris Tobias 100 E Main Street, Charlottesville, VA 22902
800-424-3950 804-296-6800 Fax 804-296-2154
Email Copernicus@1q.com   http://www.1q.com/Copernicus
Distributor Wholesale Retail Mail Order on Web Site
(Elementary School to Adult)
Ask for 12-page wholesale catalog. Member of Museum Store
Association. Geodome, Volcano, Starglow, Rootbeer Kit, Bubblegum
Kit, boomerangs, fly back plane, balloon car, Make a Clock Kit, Rattle
Back, large Swinging Wonder, Echo Mike, Radiometer, Drinking Bird,
Tornado Tube, magnifying glasses, astronaut ice cream, hand boiler,
Magic Garden, abacus, Large Dome Making Kit, glow paint, glow bugs,
spiral timer, auto compass, luminous star finder, swinging wonders.

HOBERMAN DESIGNS, INC.

450 West 15th St, Suite 502, New York, NY 10011 888-229-3653
212-647-7656 Fax 212-647-7424 Email designs@hoberman.com
http://www.hoberman.com Manufacturer (Elementary School to
Adult)
Manufacturer of Hoberman Spheres that mechanically shrink and expand
by large factors.

Instant Prehistoric
Photo Courtesy of Instant Products

INSTANT PRODUCTS INC.
Contact Jack Muenz-Winkler P O Box 33068, Louisville, KY 40232 800-862-6688   502-367-2266 Fax 502-368-6958   Manufacturer (Elementary School to Adult)
Manufacturer of capsules that dissolve into animal shapes in soft foam. For ages 5 years and above. Use these capsules to study the effect of temperature by dissolving capsules at different temperatures and measuring time variations.

JCS, INC.
P O Box 12455, Chicago, IL 60612 800-469-6653 312-226-5772 Fax 312-226-5774   Manufacturer   Distributor   Wholesale (Elementary School to Adult)
Ask for brochure. Voyage Earth labs include Volcano Adventure, Earthquake Explorer, Tornado Adventure, and Geyser Exploration. Weird Monster Science includes Shrink Putty, Power Surge, Rocket Flight Formula, Invisible Ink, Flying Things and Slime Conversion Potion. Crafty Kids series includes Foot Prints, Scribble, and Face Kit.

KIPP BROTHERS, INC.
240-242 S Meridian St, P. O. Box 157, Indianapolis, IN 46206
800-428-1153 317-634-5507 Fax 800-832-5477 Fax 317-634-5518
http://www.kippbro.com Importers Retail and Wholesale
(All Ages)
Ask for 224-page catalog. Established in 1880 this distributor specializes in inexpensive toys, novelties, carnival and party items for quantity, dozen purchases. Science items include dinosaur tattoos, animal sounds, musical toys, tops, magnetic wheels, rubber and foam balls, kaleidoscopes, bird gliders, solar radiometer, telescopes, boomerangs, magnetized marbles, flying toys, kazoos, magnifying glasses, museum quality dinosaurs, and many, many more.

KLUTZ
455 Portage Ave, Palo Alto, CA 94306-2213 800-558-8944
Fax 800-524-4075 650-424-0739 Manufacturer Retail Mail Order
(Elementary School to High School)
Ask for the 46-page Klutz Catalogue. Really fun toys and novelties. Amazon Worms, Smartballs, Smartrings, The Explorabook - a kids science museum in a book, ExploraCenter, Backyard Weather Station kit, Mega-Magnet Set, Backyard Bird Book with bird caller, The Aerobie Orbiter, Rubber Stamp Bug Kit, Vinyl Vermin, Kids Gardening Guide, World Record Paper Airplane Kit, The Arrowcopter, Megaballoons, Bubble Book, Zoetrope, juggling materials.

**Mindtrix™
Holographic Puzzle**
Photo Courtesy of Lightrix

LIGHTRIX, INC.
2132 Adams Ave, San Leandro, CA
94577   800-850-4656 510-577-7800
Fax 415-244-9795
Email   dlr@lightrix.com
http://www.lightrix.com
Manufacturer   Wholesale
(Elementary School to Adult)
Holographic toys and novelties.
Products include bright holograms of
nature & science, holographic sunglasses, Spectrix Visors, Eccentrix
diffraction discs, science puzzles,
dinosaurs, and more.

Small Stair Timers
Photo Courtesy of The Lyon Company

THE LYON COMPANY
2400 South 600 West, Salt Lake City,
UT   84115   801-972-2888   Fax
801-972-2890 Distributor (All Ages)
Ask for Lyon Motion Products catalog.
Promotional products with fluids in
motion, including many unique designs
and products.

M. RUSKIN CO.

P O Box 222, Rockaway Park, NY 11694 718-474-1680
Fax 718-474-5439 Manufacturer Wholesale (Elementary School)
Ask for brochure. Educational place mats including science subjects.

MRS. GROSSMAN'S PAPER CO.

Contact Jeff Shaw   3810 Cypress Drive, Petaluma, CA 94954
800-457-4570 707-763-1700 Fax 707-763-7121
Email jshaw@mrsgrossmans.com   http://www.mrsgrossmans.com
Manufacturer Wholesale (Elementary School)
Ask for 74-page catalog. Peel-off stickers, idea books, and kits include
topics on dinosaurs, nature, ocean life, and animals.

NATUREPRINT PAPER PRODUCTS

P O Box 314, Moraga, CA 94556 Manufacturer
(Elementary School to High School)
Natureprint paper and transparencies. This sun-sensitive paper exposes
in direct sunlight to create white on blue prints of leaf outlines or animal
picture transparencies. Expose 2-3 minutes and then develop in tapwater
in seconds.

NERD KARDS
(Names Earning Respect & Dignity) P O Box 900, Monroe, CT 06468-0900 203-925-9773 Fax 203-925-9773
Email nerdkards@snet.net   http://www.nerdkards.com
(High School to Adult)
This set of 102 Kards features scientists with their major discoveries and inventions. $ 13.45 per set.

AstroJax™
Photo Courtesy of New Toy Classics

NEW TOY CLASSICS
3627 Sacramento St, San Francisco, CA   94118   888-ASTROJA(X) 415-673-6382   Fax 415-673-6241 Manufacturer Distributor (Elementary School to High School)
Ask for brochure, and AstroJax Science Workbook. Manufacturer of AstroJax, three balls on a rubber string, that works like a yo-yo to produce orbits and other feats. This award-winning toy was invented by a physicist.

ORBIX CORPORATION
6329 Mori Street, McLean, VA 22101 703-356-0695 Manufacturer (Elementary School to Adult)
Ask for brochure. Manufacturer of Odd Balls, an educational toy made from three types of wedges assembled onto a central disk. You can use Odd Balls to demonstrate principles of geometry and physics and to teach mathematics concepts including fractions. They reassemble to make tops, pinwheels, and balls.

ORIENTAL TRADING CO., INC.

P O Box 2308, Omaha, NE 68103-2308 800-228-0122 Fax 800-228-1002 http://www.oriental.com **Distributor Wholesale Retail Mail Order (All ages)**

Reptile Bean Bags
Photo Courtesy of Oriental Trading

Ask for 180-page catalog. Source of inexpensive novelties, including magnifying glasses, plastic tops, mini reflectors, balloons, balloon helicopters, and many, many more.

PARTY PIGS

Contact Sam Armstrong 3258 Hawthorne Road, Ottawa, Ontario, Canada K1G 3W9 800-467-7447 613-739-8854 Fax 613-739-1481 Email larich@concentric.com Manufacturer Distributor Wholesale (Elementary School to High School)

Ask for 45-page catalog. Novelties in science include magnetic marbles, frog ball, snake ball, lizard ball, eye ball glow, glowing stars, glow lizards, glow frogs, rainbow maker, finger boiling pen, compasses, mineral sets, adult & young pythons, slide whistle, hatching dino eggs, and many more.

PEELEMAN-MCLAUGHLIN ENTERPRISES INC.

European Expressions, 4153 South 300 West, Murray, UT 84107 800-779-2205 Fax 801-263-2053 Manufacturer Wholesale Retail Mail Order http://www.europeanexpressions.com (Elementary School)

Ask for brochure. Science toys include Perfume Creations, Magnetic Intelligence Test, and Magnetic Fishing.

PLAY VISIONS

1137 N 96th St, Seattle, WA 98103   Contact Mario DiPasquale
800-678-8697 Fax 206-524-2766 Email mariod@playvisions.com
http://www.playvisions.com Manufacturer (Elementary School)
Ask for 50-page catalog. Telescopes, optical toys, Giant Rainforest
Insects, reptiles & amphibians, Habitat nature model sets, dinosaur toy
sets, vinyl Earth balls, Earth Squish Balls, Native American Arrowheads,
and many inexpensive novelty items.

PLAY-BY-PLAY ACE-ACME

4100 Forest Park, St. Louis, MO 63108-2899   800-325-7888
http://www.pbpus.com Importer, Manufacturer and Distributor
Retail Mail Order (All ages)
Ask for 110-page catalog filled with a very large variety of inexpensive
toys and novelties that demonstrate natural phenomena. An excellent
source for science teachers.

POOF PRODUCTS, INC.

Contact Ray Dallavecchia   45400 Helm St, P O Box 701394,
Plymouth, MI   48170-0964   800-829-9502 734-454-9552   Fax
734-454-9540 Email poof@webbernet.net http://www.poof-toys.com
Manufacturer (Elementary School to High School)
Ask for brochure. Manufacturer of soft, flying foam toys, including
basketballs, footballs, Soft Touch Yo-Yo, Soft Racers, Mega Plane,
Blasteroid Rocket with Lancher, Ramrocket, Turbospin Flying Bug,
helicopters, airplanes, kites, Foam Farm, educational puzzles, and more.

THE STRAIGHT EDGE, INC.
296 Court Street, Brooklyn, NY 11231 800-732-3628 718-643-2794 Fax 718-403-9582 Manufacturer Email straedge@aol.com (Preschool to Elementary School) Ask for 12-page catalog. Products include Color a Magnet and Read a Mat (table mat) with animals, math, and science.

Read a Mat®
Photo Courtesy of The Straight Edge

UNIVERSAL SPECIALTIES CO., INC.
7355 W Vickery Blvd, Fort Worth, TX 76116 800-728-5299 817-738-5299 Fax 817-738-2115 Distributor Wholesale (Elementary School to Adult) Ask for 30-page catalog. This distributor of inexpensive novelty items sells many toys about science or toys that demonstrate natural phenomena.

Handboilers
Photo Courtesy of Westminster Intn'l

WESTMINSTER INTERNATIONAL CO., INC.
436 Armour Circle N E, Atlanta, GA
30324 800-241-8697   404-876-6008
Fax 404-892-3471
Email toys@compuserve.com
http://www.westminsterinc.com
Manufacturer Distributor
Wholesale (Elementary School)
Ask for 16-page catalog. Fast action, fun toys including Diving Dophin, Galactic Shooter, Handboilers, Pen Boilers, Liquid Motion, Color Wave, Sandtimer, Magic Illusion Disk, Newton's Cradles, and more.

**Roller Woody and
Sleep Machine Yo Yo's**
Photo Courtesy of What's Next

WHAT'S NEXT MFG. INC.
P O Box 276, Arcade, NY 14009
800-US-YOYOS   800-458-8635
716-492-1014   Fax 716-492-1018
Manufacturer   Retail Mail Order
(Elementary School to Adult)
Ask for brochure. Manufacturer of hand crafted YO YOs and the world's longest spinning, ball bearing YO YOs.

YOMEGA CORPORATION

Contact Rose Martel 638 Quequechan St, P O Box 4146, Fall River, MA   02723-0402   800-338-8796   617-672-7399   Fax 508-677-1599 http://www.yomega.com Distributor Wholesale Retail Mail Order (Elementary School to High School)

High performance Yo-Yos including longest spinning, automatically returning, transaxle Yo-Yos, and many more. Ask for a copy of Yo-Yo Physics by Mark Lienau, an educational application to study angular dynamics.

Chapter

7   Outdoor Toys

A G INDUSTRIES
Contact Aaron Tibbs   15335 N E 95th St, Redmond, WA 98052
800-233-7174   425-885-4599   Fax 425-885-4672
Email   atibbs@whitewings.com   http://www.whitewings.com
Manufacturer Retail and Wholesale
(Elementary School to High School)
Ask for 12-page catalog. Educational kits for constructing paper airplane
gliders, boats and origami. Whitewings series includes the History of
Passenger Planes, Future of Flight, History of Jet Fighters, Racers, Space
Shuttle, Science of Flight. Display cases for home and retail stores.

ACTIVE VERMONT, INC.
P O Box 4425, White River Junction, VT 05001 888-296-RANGS
802-296-7244 Fax 802-296-7244 Email activermont@cyberportal.net
Distributor Wholesale (All Ages)
Ask for brochure. Distributor of Australian-made Boomerangs. Soft
Indoor to Polymer Sport Models.

BEAR CREEK TOYS, INC.

P O Box 247, Woodinville, WA 98072 800-232-7275 425-788-8104 Fax 425-844-2262 **Manufacturer Wholesale (Elementary School)** Ask for 8-page catalog. Science and Nature Products include Critter Catcher Gift Set, Nature Net, Activity Jar, Bones & Rocks Earth Science Kit, Treasure Adventure, Plant Patch Growing Kits, Plant Patch Shovel, and more.

CARSON & COPITAR

Contact Jeni Sikorski 200 E Second St, Unit 5, Huntington Station, NY 11746 800-967-8427 516-427-6570 Fax 516-427-6749 Email jsikorski@carson-optical.com http://carson-optical.com Manufacturer (Elementary School to Adult) Ask for brochures. Manufacturer of binoculars, magnifiers, telescopes, and a wide variety of quality optical instruments, including X-Scope, a multi-use optical pocket tool.

Copitar Light-Up MINI Binocular Photo Courtesy of Carson & Copitar

Celestron Telescope
Photo Courtesy of Celestron Intn'l

CELESTRON INTERNATIONAL
Contact Linda Waible 2835 Columbia St, Torrance, CA 90503 310-328-9560 Fax 310-212-5835 Email l_waible@celestron.com http://www.celestron.com Manufacturer Distributor (High School to Adult)
Ask for catalogs: Telescopes for Astron-omy, Celestron Telescopes, Celestron Binoculars & Spotting Scopes, Lab Grade Microscopes, and Celestron Accessories. Major manufacturer of telescopes.

CHANNEL CRAFT & DIST. INC.
P O Box 101, North Charleroi, PA 15022 800-232-4FUN 412-489-4900 Fax 412-489-0773 http://www.channelcraft.com Manufacturer Distributor Wholesale (Elementary School to Adult)
Ask for 35-page catalog. Quality wooden toys, puzzles, and games made in USA, including Yo-Yo's, Jacob's Ladder, Boomerangs, Tops, Brain Teaser, Mind Bogglers, and more.

CHUTE-N-STAR
1480 Pinyon Place, Lawrenceville, GA 30043 Contact John Henly, Vice President, Sales 770-962-5361 Fax 770-962-5361 Manufacturer (Elementary School to Adult)
Ask for brochure. Manufacturer of Chute-N-Star, a pocket-fitting, flying, bouncing toy with pentagon shape and five rubber balls.

DAVIS LIQUID CRYSTALS INC.

15021 Wicks Blvd, San Leandro, CA 94577   800-677-5575
Fax 510-351-2328   Manufacturer Distributor Wholesale
(Elementary School to Adult)
Manufacturer of liquid crystal novelties that change color when touched. Products include SolarZone T-shirts with science designs that change from indoor black and white to outdoor full color.

Solarzone™ T-Shirts
Photo Courtesy of
Davis Liquid Crystals

EDMUND SCIENTIFIC COMPANY

101 E Gloucester Pike, Barrington, NJ 08007-1380
800-728-6999   609-573-3488   Fax 609-573-6272
http://www.edsci.com Retail (All ages)
Ask for 112-page science reference catalog for educators. Since 1942 this well known scientific optical supplier also sells many other items including lasers, microscopes, camera/monitor systems, science classroom anatomy models, nature kits, laboratory safety equipment, balances, weather instruments, timers, magnets, small motors & pumps, robot kits, earth science kits, telescopes, museum animal replicas, and unique classroom materials for teachers.

ENVIRO-MENTAL TOY CO. INC.

P O Box 580186, Flushing, NY 11358 718-428-8972 Manufacturer Distributor Wholesale (All Ages)
Ask for brochure. Products include Sun-Sational Science Tee Shirts with natural science animal pictures that are black & white indoors, but instantly change to full color when exposed to sunshine. Indoors they fade back to black & white.

X-Ray™ Estes Rocket
Photo Courtesy of Estes Industries

ESTES INDUSTRIES

Contact Ann Grimm 1295 H Street, Penrose, CO 81240 800-820-0202 Fax 800-820-0203   719-372-3217 Manufacturer   Retail to teachers. (High School to Adult)
Ask for Estes Educator Catalog on school letterhead.   Supplies model rockets, engines, accessories, and curricula.

FREUD, MORRIS & WILLIAMS

200 Fifth Ave, Suite 835, New York, NY 10010   Distributor (Elementary School)
Ask for 15-page catalog. Distributor of Science Tech microscopes, telescopes, binoculars, videoscope, anatomical models, magnets, periscopes, chemistry lab kit, magnifier, bug viewer, stereoscope, and more.

GALT AMERICA

Distributor of GALT Toys, 230 Woodmont Road, Milford, CT 06460
800-899-4258 Fax 203-876-2739 http://www.galt-co.uk Distributor
Wholesale (Preschool to Elementary School)
Ask for 56-page catalog. These well-known toys are Made-in-United
Kingdom. Science toys include Seasonal Puzzles, Water Puzzles, Marble
Run, Magnet Building, Connecta-Straws, Young Explorer series,
Telescope, Microscope, Binoculars, Crystal Radio Kit, Intruder Alarm
Kit, Electrical Games Kit, Bug Watch Kit, Ecology Kit, and more.

I.G.C. GIOCATTOLI MAX SAS

Zona Instriale 43, Lanchiano, C H, Italy 0872-42205 Fax 0872-43281
Manufacturer Wholesale (Elementary School to High School)
Ask for 44-page catalog. Quality microscope kits, microscope monitors,
gardening kits, chemistry sets, and telescopes.

KIPP BROTHERS, INC.

240-242 S Meridian St, P. O. Box 157, Indianapolis, IN 46206
800-428-1153 317-634-5507 Fax 800-832-5477 Fax 317-634-5518
http:// www.kippbro.com Importers Retail and Wholesale
(All Ages)
Ask for 224-page catalog. Established in 1880 this distributor specializes
in inexpensive toys, novelties, carnival and party items for quantity,
dozen purchases. Science items include dinosaur tattoos, animal sounds,
musical toys, tops, magnetic wheels, rubber and foam balls,
kaleidoscopes, bird gliders, solar radiometer, telescopes, boomerangs,
magnetized marbles, flying toys, kazoos, magnifying glasses, museum
quality dinosaurs, and many, many more.

KLUTZ

455 Portage Ave, Palo Alto, CA 94306-2213 800-558-8944
Fax 800-524-4075 650-424-0739 Manufacturer Retail Mail Order
(Elementary School to High School)
Ask for the 46-page Klutz Catalogue. Really fun toys and novelties.
Amazon Worms, Smartballs, Smartrings, The Explorabook - a kids
science museum in a book, ExploraCenter, Backyard Weather Station kit,
Mega-Magnet Set, Backyard Bird Book with bird caller, The Aerobie
Orbiter, Rubber Stamp Bug Kit, Vinyl Vermin, Kids Gardening Guide,
World Record Paper Airplane Kit, The Arrowcopter, Megaballoons,
Bubble Book, Zoetrope, juggling materials.

Mead 16" Lx200 Telescope
Photo Courtesy of Meade Instruments

MEADE INSTRUMENTS CORP.

6001 Oak Canyon, Irvine, CA
92620-4205   949-451-1450
Fax 949-451-1460
http://www.meade.com
Manufacturer   Distributor
(Elementary School to College)
Ask for 102-page catalog. Quality
optical telescopes, binoculars, and
spotting scopes.

MIDWEST MODEL SUPPLY CO.

12040 S Aero Dr, Plainfield, IL 60544 800-573-7029 815-254-2151
Fax 815-254-2445   Email mwmodelsup@aol.com   Distributor
Wholesale Quantity School Orders. (Elementary School to College)
Ask for literature. Source for Estes Rockets & accessories, bridge
building kits, aero-space models, plane programs, mousetrap racers, and
model making materials.

MORE BALLS THAN MOST

Contact Virginia Wages-Plotkin 26 W 17th St, # 702, New York, NY 10011   800-544-3688, ext 13 212-691-9660, ext 13 Fax   212-691-9633   Email Virginia@MBTMNY.mhs.compuse rve.com Manufacturer Distributor Wholesale (Elementary School to Adult)

The Rokit
Photo Courtesy of
More Balls than Most

Ask for 20-page catalog. Toys include hot air balloon kits, The Rokit (launch a soda bottle up to 50 feet with compressed air), Buster Bloodvessel (wooden and wire puzzles), Optical (pocket optical illusion jigsaw), Penultimate (a pen that floats on air and spins on a frictionless bed), juggling supplies, and more.

OZWEST INC

P O Box 747, Banks, OR 97106 503-324-8018 Fax 503-324-2016 Email ozwest@aol.com Manufacturer Distributor Wholesale (Elementary School to High School)
Ask for brochure. Manufacturer of flying toys: Flipz, Roomarang, Super Roomarang, Holarang, Wood Boomarangs, Fling Ring.

PLAY VISIONS

1137 N 96th St, Seattle, WA 98103 Contact Mario DiPasquale 800-678-8697 Fax 206-524-2766 Email mariod@playvisions.com http://www.playvisions.com Manufacturer (Elementary School) Ask for 50-page catalog. Telescopes, optical toys, Giant Rainforest Insects, reptiles & amphibians, Habitat nature model sets, dinosaur toy sets, vinyl Earth balls, Earth Squish Balls, Native American Arrowheads, and many inexpensive novelty items.

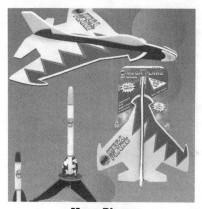

Mega Plane™
Photo Courtesy of Poof Products

POOF PRODUCTS, INC.
Contact Ray Dallavecchia   45400 Helm St, P O Box 701394, Plymouth, MI 48170-0964   800-829-9502 734-454-9552 Fax 734-454-9540 Email poof@webbernet.net http://www.poof-toys.com **Manufacturer (Elementary School to High School)**
Ask for brochure. Manufacturer of soft, flying foam toys, including basketballs, footballs, Soft Touch Yo-Yo, Soft Racers, Mega Plane, Blasteroid Rocket with Lancher, Ramrocket, Turbospin Flying Bug, helicopters, airplanes, kites, Foam Farm, educational puzzles, and more.

X-30 National Aerospace Plane
Photo Courtesy of Quest Aerospace

QUEST AEROSPACE
A division of Toy Biz, Inc. 350 East 18th St, Yuma, AZ   85364 800-858-7302 ext 110 **Manufacturer Retail Mail Order (High School)**
Ask for 35-page catalog. Rockets and accessories for model rocketry.

SAKAR INTERNATIONAL INC.

195 Carter Drive, Edison, NJ 08817
800-637-1090   732-248-1306
Fax 732-248-1796   Manufacturer
Wholesale
(Elementary School to Adult)
Manufacturer of optical products
including cameras and binoculars.

Sakar 10x50mm Binocular
Photo Courtesy of Sakar Intn'l

SCIENTIFIC EXPLORER, INC.

4020 E Madison, Suite 326, Seattle, WA   98112 800-900-1182
206-322-7611 Fax 206-322-7610 Email sciex@scientificexplorer.com
http://www.scientificexplorer.com   http://www.gettoys.com
Manufacturer Retail Mail Order (Elementary School to Adult)
Ask for 16-page catalog. Manufacturer of science and adventure kits
including Fun with Your Cat, Fun with Your Dog, Smithsonian
Adventures Series, Aerial Camera, High Altitude Launcher, Science of
Scent, Make Animal Soaps, Kitchen Science, Educational Cooking
Center, Nature Adventures, Exploring Electronics, Science of Sound, and
many more.

SELSI COMPANY, INC.

P O Box 10, 194 Greenwood Ave, Midland Park, NJ 07432-0010
800-275-7357   201-612-9200   Fax 201-612-9548   Manufacturer
Wholesale (Elementary School to Adult)
Quality binoculars, telescopes, student microscope sets, magnifiers, toy
kaleidoscopes, glass prisms, student magnets, compasses, barometers,
altimeters, metal detectors.

SKY PUBLISHING CORP.

Sky Publishing Corp., 49 Bay State Rd, Cambridge, MA 02138 / Sky
& Telescope, P O Box 9111, Belmont, MA 02178-9111 800-253-0245
617-864-7360   Fax 617-864-6117   Email skytel@skypub.com
http://www.skypub.com Since 1941. (High School to College)
Ask for 32-page catalog of products for professional and amateur
astronomers. Products include maps, books, videos, globes, posters,
software, CD-ROMs, slide sets, star atlases, and planispheres.

SUPERFLIGHT, INC.

Contact Alex Tennant   81 Encina Ave, Palo Alto, CA   94301
650-321-5050 Fax 650-321-0974 Manufacturer
(Elementary School to High School)
Ask for brochure. Manufacturer of aerodynamic flying toys, Aerobie
brand products and the Squidgie Ball. The Aerobie Pro Flying Ring
holds the Guinness World Record for the farthest throw, 1,257 feet or
over four football fields.

TASCO
2889 Commerce Parkway, Miramar, FL 33025 / P O Box 269000, Pembroke Pines, FL 33026
888-GET-TASCO   954-252-3600
Fax 954-252-3705
http://www.tascosales.com
Manufacturer Distributor
(Elementary School to Adult)
Ask for 52-page Recreational Optics catalog. Quality optical products for all ages. Children's products include Big Screen Microscope, Binoculars, Periscopes, Magnifiers and more.

TASCO® Periscope
Photo Courtesy of TASCO

Adult products include Lasersite Range-finder, Night Watch Viewing Optics, Binoculars, Zoom Binoculars, Sport Telescopes, Astronomical Telescopes, and more.

TWC OF AMERICA, INC
Contact Terry Weber 9663 Hwy 144 North, Kewaskum, WI 53040
800-301-7592 414-692-6835 Fax 414-692-6709
http://www.twcoa.com   http://www.tweber.com   Manufacturer
Wholesale (Elementary School to Adult)
Ask for 8-page TWC Gifts Catalog, including quality products for nature lovers: Insect & Pond Nets, various wooden Nature Houses, bat houses, OBE II Bird Feeder, Colonial Birdhouse Kits. Ask for 8-page Tweber Backyard Explorer Gear Catalog, including products for the young nature lover: Play Tent, Nature Houses, Nature Exploring & Catch-All Nets, Butterfly Loft, Leaf Press, Bird Houses, and Bird Feeders.

VAN CORT INSTRUMENTS, INC.

12 Greenfield Rd, P O Box 215, South Deerfield, MA 01373-0215
800-432-2678 413-586-9800 Fax 413-665-2300
Email sales@vancort.com http://www.vancort.com Manufacturer
Wholesale Retail Mail Order (Elementary School to Adult)
Ask for catalog. Manufacturer of quality telescopes, kaleidoscopes, timepieces, magnifying glasses, and unique instruments including the toy, U-ME, an optical illusion mirror that combines faces. Products handmade in New England.

WILD PLANET TOYS

Contact Molly McCahan 98 Battery Street, Suite 300, San Francisco, CA 94111 800-247-6570 415-705-8300 Fax 415-705-8311
Email mccahan@wildplanet.com http://www.wildplanet.com
Manufacturer (Elementary School to Middle School)
Wild Planet Toys manufacture a series of fun investigative toys demonstrating that technology is simply an extension of the human body for observation and communication. Toys include Electronic Gaget Set, Hands-Free Walkie Talkie, Radio Watch, Night Scope Binoculars, Wrist Talkies, Body Mike, Signal Watch, Sonic Scope, Metal Detector, Sleuth Scope, Supersonic Ear, and many more.

WILLIAM MARK CORP.
Contact Mark Forti 112 N Harvard Ave, Suite 229, Claremont, CA 91711 800-604-0030 909-621-6823 Fax 909-621-4247
Email mforti@aol.com
http://www.x-zylo.com
Manufacturer
(Elementary School to Adult)
Ask for brochure. Manufacturer of X-Zylo, the Amazing Flying Gyroscope. Incredibly thrown like a football for over 200 yards! A new technology of flight.

X-Zylo
Photo Courtesy of William Mark Corp.

Chapter

8 Preschool & Infant Toys

ALPI INTERNATIONAL LTD.
P O Box 8835, Emeryville, CA 94662 800-678-ALPI 510-655-6456
Fax 510-655-2093 http://www.alpi.net Manufacturer Wholesale
(Preschool to Elementary School)
Ask for 38-page catalog. Squeezable preschool toys including famous
characters, animals of all varieties, dinosaurs, and more. Also, Glow in
the Dark chalk, paint, and toys. Many science toys including Star Finder,
Optic Wonder, gyroscopes, and more.

ANATEX ENTERPRISES

15929 Arminta St, Van Nuys, CA 91406 800-999-9599 818-908-1888
Fax 818-908-0656 Email anatex@anatex.com
http://www.anatex.com Manufacturer Distributor
(Preschool to Primary)
Ask for 24-page catalog. Quality toys for preschoolers that encourage the development of both cognitive and motor skills. Products include Magnetic Bug Life Table, Ten Counter, Fleur Rollercoaster Table, Cyclone, Wonder Bug Mazes, Magnetooli, Pathfinder, Shape 'n' Color Coaster, and more.

DEXTER EDUCATIONAL TOYS, INC.

P O Box 630861, Miami, FL 33163
305-931-7426 Fax 305-931-0552
Manufacturer Wholesale
(Preschool to Elementary School)
Ask for brochure. Manufacturer of creative career role playing costumes and puppets, including The Scientist, The Teacher, The Police Officer, and many more. Ask about local distributor or purchase on school letterhead.

Career Dressups
Photo Courtesy of
Dexter Educational Toys

ECO-BRAZIL CORP.
Contact Elizabeth Howitt 250 West 94th Street, #13J, New York, NY
10025 800-272-3811 212-222-1285 Fax 212-222-1154
Manufacturer Wholesale Retail (Elementary School)
Ask for brochure. Manufacturer of soft, colorful Moving Masks: Shark,
Elephant, Frog, Bird, Alligator, Wolf, Lion, Dragon, Monkey, and
Rabbit. Also soft, colorful Funny Bugs puppets: Grasshopper, Spider,
Bee, and Lady Bug. As well as Mobiles, small Hand Puppets, and Finger
Puppets.

EDUCA SALLENT S. A.
**Osona, 1, 08192 Sant Quirze Del Valles, Barcelona, Spain
343-721-6831 Fax 343-721-6830 Manufacturer (Preschool)**
Manufacturer of quality puzzles. Educational preschool puzzles in wood
include Contrasts; Learning about series: My Body, The Months of the
Year, The Four Seasons, From 1 to 10, The Animals, The Days of the
Week; and more.

Roger Rocket™
Photo Courtesy of Educo Intn'l

EDUCO INTERNATIONAL INC.
**Contact Colleen Madsen 123 Cree
Road, Sherwood Park, Alberta,
Canada T8A 3X9 800-661-4142
403-467-9772 Fax 403-467-4014
Email mazes@educo.com
http://www.educo.com Manufacturer
(Preschool)**
Ask for 20-page catalog. Manufacturer
of quality bead-on-wire mazes. Science
related portable mazes include Tyler
Turtle, Roger Rocket, and Freddie Fish.
Also Time Catcher, where kids collect
treasures in their own time capsule.

ELWOOD TURNER CO.

HC39 Box 132, Morrisville, VT 05661   802-888-3375
Fax 802-888-3155   Email turnertoys@aol.com
http://www.turnertoys.com **Manufacturer Distributor Wholesale**
Retail Mail Order (Preschool)
Ask for catalog. Manufacturer of Quarks Creative Buiding System:
Building Toy for 3-Year-Olds. This toy is also found on the desks of
architects, artists, and engineers. Innovative wooden toys since 1979.

GUIDECRAFT USA

P O Box 324/Industrial Center, Garnerville, NY   10923-0324
800-544-6526 914-947-3500 Fax 914-947-3770
Email Gdcraft324@aol.com **Manufacturer Distributor**
Retail Mail Order (Preschool to Elementary School)
Ask for 16-page catalog. Fine wooden toys that teach, including Clock
Puzzle House, Fax Machine, Mini-Animal Puzzles, Time Sequencing,
Wooden Educational Games, 3-D Fruit & Vegetable Puzzles, Career Sets,
and Alligator Pull Toy.

HARRISON COONEY, INC.

Early Childhood Specialists, 9827 W Farragut, Chicago, IL 60018
773-992-0940 Fax 773-992-0944 Distributor
(Preschool and Elementary School)
Ask for 130-page catalog. Products include furniture to manipulatives for
preschool and primary school.

HUGG-A-PLANET

Contact Patricia Howard 247 Rockingstone Ave, Larchmont, NY 10538 914-833-0200 Fax 914-833-0303 Email Hugaword@aol.com http://www.Hugg-A-Planet.com Manufacturer
(Preschool to Elementary School)
Ask for brochure. Soft Earth globes and maps, including Hugg-A-Planet, Geophysical with no political boundaries, Hugg-America, Hugg-A-Star celestial sphere, and Hugg-A-Planet Mars.

JUMP START DEVELOPMENTAL PLAY PRODUCTS

Contact Aubrey Carton Belle Curve Records, Inc., P O Box 18387, Boulder, CO 80308 888-357-5867 303-494-7540 Fax 303-494-7555 Email at http://www.hopskipjumpstart.com http://bellecurve.com Manufacturer Distributor Wholesale
(Preschool and Elementary School)
Ask for brochure. Tapes, CDs and parent-friendly books introduce kids with sensory-motor, developmental, and social-emotional challenges.

LITTLE KIDS, INC.

Contact Jim Engle 222 Richmond St, Suite 302, Providence, RI 02903 800-545-5437 401-454-7600 Fax 401-455-0630
Manufacturer (Elementary School)
Ask for catalog. Science related toys include many various bubble-making toys and realistically styled plush animals that make sounds from actual animals.

THE LITTLE TIKES COMPANY

2180 Barlow Road, P O Box 2277, Hudson, OH 44236 800-321-0183 http://www.littletikes.com Manufacturer Distributor (Preschool) Ask for 25-page catalog that lists retail stores. Preschool toys and furniture that include Might Explorer Sea Sub, and Racing Roller Coasters.

THE LIVING & LEARNING CO.

1632 Curtis Street, Berkeley, CA 94702   800-306-3013 Fax 510-527-9212 Orders: 4383 Hecktown Rd, Ste GA-1, Bethlehem, PA 10820 800-521-3218 Fax 800-582-8268 Manufacturer Wholesale (Preschool to Elementary School) Ask for 14-page Science Pre-School Puzzles catalog. Products also include Jam Jar Science-Bugs (Bug collecting), Where in the Wild? (Game), Explore! (Game), and many more.

Science in the Bathtub Kit
Photo Courtesy of
Living & Learning Co.

NORTHERN GIFTS INC.

Contact Bob MacKerricher 250-H Street, P O Box 8110-882, Blaine, WA   98231   800-665-0808   604-299-5050   Fax 604-299-0808 Manufacturer Wholesale Retail Mail Order (Elementary School) Ask for 16-page catalog. Manufacturer of Canned Critters, plush toys sealed in a can with a complete description of each animal as it appears in nature. Canned Critters include Canned Black Bear, Moose, Sea Turtle, Raccoon, Buffalo, Beaver, Wolf, Loon, Bald Eagle, Penguin, Owl, Bat, Armadillo, Alligator, and many more.

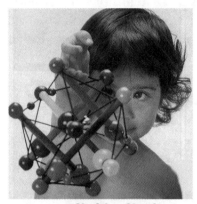

Skwish® Classic
Photo Courtesy of
Pappa Geppetto's Toys

PAPPA GEPPETTO'S TOYS VICTORIA LTD.

P O Box 3567, Blaine, WA 98231-3567   800-667-5407
Fax 800-973-5678   250-382-9975
Email   pappa@mail.islandnet.com
Manufacturer (Toys for Baby as well as All Ages)
Manufacturer of Skwish Classic, mobile Tranquility V, Wooden Mini Dinosaurs, and Flex-Bugs.

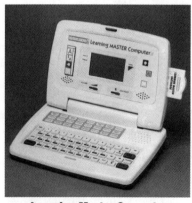

Learning Master Computer™
Photo Courtesy of Play-Tech

PLAY-TECH, INC.

Contact Maryann Raphael 200 Fifth Ave, Suite 1452, New York, NY 10010   212-242-3020
Fax 212-242-3087   **Manufacturer Distributor Wholesale
(Preschool and Elementary School)**
Ask for brochures. IQ Builder's Early Learning Aids and Infant/Preschool Toys, Little Tikes Preschool Electronic Toys, Capsela Construction Toys.

SAFESPACE CONCEPTS, INC.

Contact Barbara Carlson, Ph.D. 1424 North Post Oak, Houston, TX 77055 800-622-4289 713-956-0820 Fax 713-956-6416 Email SafeSpaceC@aol.com Manufacturer Retail Mail Order (Preschool to Elementary School) Ask for 6-page catalog. Manufacturer of creative soft furniture for young children.

Motion Complex Play Set
Photo Courtesy of Safespace Concepts

SENTOSPHERE USA

81 E Second St, New York, NY 10003 212-674-8202 Fax 212-505-9526 Manufacturer Wholesale (Elementary School) Ask for brochure. Products include Follow Your Nose (a game with 30 distinct aroma samples), Perfume Maker (chemically create more than 100 different fragrances), and many preschool wood puzzles of nature and science.

TREE BLOCKS

Contact Terri Smith=Oppen 21103 Mulholland Dr, Woodland Hills, CA 91364 800-873-4960 818-992-4569 Fax 818-348-9639 Email elves@treeblocks.com http://www.treeblocks.com Manufacturer (Preschool to Elementary School) Tree Blocks are building blocks cut from smooth real tree branches. Using these building blocks one feels the complexity of nature.

Tree Blocks™
Photo Courtesy of Tree Blocks

USTOY CONSTRUCTIVE PLAYTHINGS
1227 E 119th St, Gradview, MO 64030-1117 800-448-4115
816-761-5900   Fax 816-761-9295   Email ustoy@ustoyco.com
http://www.ustoyco.com Manufacturer Distributor Wholesale
Retail Mail Order (Preschool to Elementary School)
Ask for 200-page catalog filled with educational fun for the preschool and
elementary school age child including six pages of hands-on science
materials.

W J FANTASY INC.
Contact John McGrath 955 Connecticut Ave, Bridgeport, CT 06607
800-222-7529   203-333-5212   Fax 203-366-3826   Distributor
Wholesale (Elementary School)
Building blocks for young children including Mini Bug Blocks,
Endangered Wild Life Blocks, and Farmyard Friends.

Chapter

9

Puzzles

ARK FOUNDATION
34 Smith St, Norwalk, CN 06851
888-ARK-8500   914-421-2195
Fax 203-855-7660
http://www.arkfoundation.com
**Manufacturer Retail mail order
(Elementary School to High School)**
Manufacturer of Preservation Puzzles,
large and colorful foam puzzles of rare,
exotic and often endangered species.

Preservation Puzzles™
Photo Courtesy of Ark Foundation

Brain Bending™ Puzzles
Photo Courtesy of B. Dazzle

B. DAZZLE, INC.
500 Meyer Lane, Redondo Beach, CA 90278 310-374-3000
Fax 310-318-6692
Email info@b-dazzle.com
http://www.b-dazzle.com
Manufacturer Wholesale
(Elementary School)
Ask for 12-page Scramble Squares catalog. These brain-bending puzzles are two-dimensional, nine-piece, and illustrated. Science theme puzzles include Frogs, Penguins, Water Birds, Bats, Butterflies, Tropical Fish, Bears, Birds of Prey, Dolphins, Insects, Sharks, and many more.

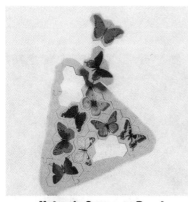

Nature's Spaces™ Puzzles
Photo Courtesy of Binary Arts

BINARY ARTS CORP.
Contact Jennifer Koshute 1321 Cameron St, Alexandria, VA 22314
800-468-1864 703-549-4999
Fax 703-549-6210
Email jkoschute@puzzles.com
http://www.puzzles.com
Manufacturer Distributor
Wholesale
(Elementary School to Adult)
Ask for 20-page catalog. Award winning games and puzzles include Rush Hour 2, Visual Brainstorms, Port to Port, Block by Block, Brick by Brick, Back-Spin, Top-Spin, Switch Back, Spin-Out, Nature's Spaces, Izzi, and many more. Thinking toys.

CHANNEL CRAFT & DIST. INC.

P O Box 101, North Charleroi, PA 15022 800-232-4FUN 412-489-4900 Fax 412-489-0773 http://www.channelcraft.com Manufacturer Distributor Wholesale (Elementary School to Adult) Ask for 35-page catalog. Quality wooden toys, puzzles, and games made in USA, including Yo-Yo's, Jacob's Ladder, Boomerangs, Tops, Brain Teaser, Mind Bogglers, and more.

Children of the Sun Book
Photo Courtesy of Channel Craft

CURIOSITY KITS

P O Box 811, Hunt Valley, MD 21031 800-584-KITS 410-584-2605 Fax 410-584-1247 Email ckitsinc@aol.com Manufacturer Retail Mail Order (Elementary School) Ask for 28-page Kids Can Catalog. Explore the adventures in science with these Curiosity Kits: Bouncing Zoom Balls, Super Dooper Bouncing Zoom Balls, Kaleidoscope, National Geographic/Curiosity Kits: Solar System Puzzle and Coral Reef Window Aquarium, Natural Soap Making, Vision Collision, Glow-in-the-Dark Human Skeleton, and many more.

DAMERT COMPANY

1609 4th Street, Berkeley, CA 94710 800-231-3722 510-524-7400
Fax 510-524-4466 Email damert@aol.com http://www.damert.com
Manufacturer Wholesale (Elementary School to Adult)
Ask for 36-page catalog. Science toys include 3-D Slide Puzzles, Jungle
Bungles puzzles, Concentra puzzle, Tiazzle Puzzles, Master Triazzles,
coffee mugs, bulletin boards, many science mobiles, StarShines
astronomy stickers, diffraction toys, Laser Top, Spiral Mobiles, Turbo
Sparkler YoYo, liquid crystal toys and novelties, Little Critter
Kaleidoscope, Butterflies of the World, bird feeder kit, Zoetrope, Vector
Flexor, Echo Rocket, Spacephones, Tornado Tube, science charts and
posters.

DESIGN SCIENCE TOYS LTD.

Contact Don Rimsky 1362 Route 9, Tivoli, NY 12583 800-227-2316
914-756-4221 Fax 914-756-4223 Manufacturer Retail (Preschool to
Adult)
Ask for 10-page catalog. Wooden puzzles: Pyrra, Soma, Rhoma, Vexa,
Magna, Cube Octa, Quadrhom, Tetra, Dodeca. Puzzles and games:
Chung Toi, Smile Tiles-Bananas. Manipulatives: Heaven's orb,
Heaven's Pendant, Rhomblocks, Feebee, Wacbee, Turnabout, Rhomtop.
Construction toys: Tensegritoy, Stik-Trix, Roger's Connection,
Zometool. Projects: Globe Project, Octabug, Geodazzlers, Synergy Ball.

EDUCA SALLENT S. A.

Osona, 1, 08192 Sant Quirze Del Valles, Barcelona, Spain
343-721-6831 Fax 343-721-6830
Manufacturer (Preschool)
Manufacturer of quality puzzles. Educational preschool puzzles in wood include Contrasts; Learning about series: My Body, The Months of the Year, The Four Seasons, From 1 to 10, The Animals, The Days of the Week; and more.

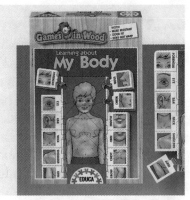

Learning About My Body Game
Photo Courtesy of Educa Sallent

EXPLORATORIUM STORE

3601 Lyon St, San Francisco, CA 94123 415-561-0393
http://www.exploratorium.edu Retail Mail Order (All ages)
See web page that is filled with quality science toys and books, including the following toys: Megabubbles Kit, The Kaleidoscope Book and Kit, Zoetrope, Wild Wood, Magnetron, Gyros, Curiosity Box, Eagle Microscope, Mirage Maker, Micro-Bank, Erector Sets, Paradox 3-D Jigsaw Puzzle, and Ellipto.

FAMILY GAMES INC.

P O Box 97, Snowdon, Montreal, Canada H3X-3T3 800-291-1176
514-485-1834 Fax 514-485-2944 Manufacturer Wholesale
(Elementary School)
Ask for 18-page catalog. Educational games, puzzles, and activities. Science products include MoonDust (paint natures creatures with colored powder), Too Cool Kit Mad Scientist Party, Tantrix award-winning puzzles and games, and more.

GALT AMERICA

Distributor of GALT Toys, 230 Woodmont Road, Milford, CT 06460
800-899-4258 Fax 203-876-2739 http://www.galt-co.uk Distributor
Wholesale (Preschool to Elementary School)
Ask for 56-page catalog. These well-known toys are Made-in-United
Kingdom. Science toys include Seasonal Puzzles, Water Puzzles, Marble
Run, Magnet Building, Connecta-Straws, Young Explorer series,
Telescope, Microscope, Binoculars, Crystal Radio Kit, Intruder Alarm
Kit, Electrical Games Kit, Bug Watch Kit, Ecology Kit, and more.

GEOSPACE PRODUCTS COMPANY

Contact Mitch Hamilton 1546 N W Woodbine Way, Seattle, WA
98177 800-800-5090 206-365-5241 Fax 206-365-5241
Email debink@spingames.com   http://www.spingames.com
Manufacturer Wholesale and Retail (Elementary School to Adult)
Magnetic marble toys, magnetic levitation games, magnetic building sets,
and spin games, including Puzzle Spin - M. C. Escher Collection.

GUIDECRAFT USA

P O Box 324/Industrial Center, Garnerville, NY   10923-0324
800-544-6526 914-947-3500 Fax 914-947-3770
Email Gdcraft324@aol.com Manufacturer Distributor
Retail Mail Order (Preschool to Elementary School)
Ask for 16-page catalog. Fine wooden toys that teach, including Clock
Puzzle House, Fax Machine, Mini-Animal Puzzles, Time Sequencing,
Wooden Educational Games, 3-D Fruit & Vegetable Puzzles, Career Sets,
and Alligator Pull Toy.

K & M INTERNATIONAL
1955 Midway Drive, Twinsburg, OH 44087 800-800-9678
216-963-8678 Fax 216-425-3777 Manufacturer Wholesale
(Elementary School to Adult)
Anatomically accurate stuffed and molded animals creatures of nature.
Stuffed products include National Geographic WildLife Ledgends, AZA
Animals, Maddalena Series, African Animals, Rainforest Animals,
Animals of the World, North American Animals, Aquaic Animals,
puppets, and more. Molded products include containers of small,
hand-held animal toys and numerous varieties of kits, puzzles, stickers,
and more.

KADON ENTERPRISES, INC.
Contact Kate Jones 1227 Lorene Dr, Suite 16, Pasadena, MD 21122
410-437-2163 Email kadon@gamepuzzles.com
http://www.gamepuzzles.com Manufacturer Retail
(Elementary School to Adult)
Ask for 15-page catalog of Gamepuzzles: for the Joy of Thinking. This
company specializes in sophisticated games and puzzles for the creative
thinker.

KINGDOM PUZZLES
7321 Vanalden Ave, Reseda, CA
91335 Fax 800-647-9989
818-705-4572 Fax 818-705-2480
Manufacturer Distributor
Wholesale Retail Mail Order
(Elementary School to Adult)
Ask for 20-page World Wildwife
Catalog. Numerous quality color
puzzles of nature's creatures.

World Wildlife Puzzles
Photo Courtesy of Kingdom Puzzles

KOLBE CONCEPTS, INC.

P O Box 15667, Phoenix, AZ 85060 602-840-9770 Fax 602-952-2706
http://www.kolbe.com **Manufacturer Retail (All ages)**
Ask for brochure. Think-ercises, Glop Shop - inventor's assortment, Go
Power - science experiments, Using Your Senses, Solar Power Winners
- experiment book, Decide & Design - inventor's book.

LIGHTRIX, INC.

2132 Adams Ave, San Leandro, CA   94577   800-850-4656
510-577-7800 Fax 415-244-9795 Email dlr@lightrix.com
http://www.lightrix.com **Manufacturer   Wholesale (Elementary
School to Adult)**
Holographic toys and novelties. Products include bright holograms of
nature & science, holographic sunglasses, Spectrix Visors, Eccentrix
diffraction discs, science puzzles, dinosaurs, and more.

THE LIVING & LEARNING CO.

1632 Curtis Street, Berkeley, CA   94702 800-306-3013   Fax
510-527-9212 Orders: 4383 Hecktown Rd, Ste GA-1, Bethlehem, PA
10820 800-521-3218 Fax 800-582-8268 **Manufacturer Wholesale
(Preschool to Elementary School)**
Ask for 14-page Science Pre-School Puzzles catalog. Products also
include Jam Jar Science-Bugs (Bug collecting), Where in the Wild?
(Game), Explore! (Game), and many more.

MINDWARE
2720 Patton Rd, Roseville, MN 55113-1138 800-999-0398
Fax 888-299-9273 Retail Mail Order (All Ages)
Ask for 40-page catalog. Products include many science toys, puzzles, and games.

ORBIX CORPORATION
6329 Mori Street, McLean, VA 22101 703-356-0695 Manufacturer (Elementary School to Adult)
Ask for brochure. Manufacturer of Odd Balls, an educational toy made from three types of wedges assembled onto a central disk. You can use Odd Balls to demonstrate principles of geometry and physics and to teach mathematics concepts including fractions. They reassemble to make tops, pinwheels, and balls.

POOF PRODUCTS, INC.
Contact Ray Dallavecchia   45400 Helm St, P O Box 701394, Plymouth, MI 48170-0964 800-829-9502 734-454-9552
Fax 734-454-9540   Email poof@webbernet.net
http://www.poof-toys.com Manufacturer (Elementary School to High School)
Ask for brochure. Manufacturer of soft, flying foam toys, including basketballs, footballs, Soft Touch Yo-Yo, Soft Racers, Mega Plane, Blasteroid Rocket with Lancher, Ramrocket, Turbospin Flying Bug, helicopters, airplanes, kites, Foam Farm, educational puzzles, and more.

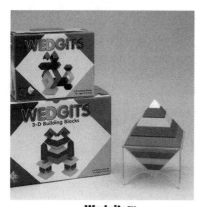

Wedgits™
Photo Courtesy of R/C Products

R/C PRODUCTS
P O Box 127, Pleasanton, CA 94566
510-846-1767   Fax 510-846-1855
Email rockmck@pacbell.net
h t t p : / / w w w . w e d g i t s . c o m
Manufacturer (Elementary School to Adult)
Wedgits is a construction toy of wedged shapes from an original cube. It teaches spatial skills and is great creative fun. Ages 3 to 103.

SAFARI LTD.
Museum Quality Creative Toys, P O Box 630685, Miami, FL 33163
800-554-5414   305-621-1000   Fax 800-766-7841
http://www.safariltd.com   Distributor Wholesale (All Ages)
129-page catalog is filled with quality science toys, including animal replicas, activities, puzzles, science toys, woodcraft, games, and posters.

SENTOSPHERE USA
81 E Second St, New York, NY 10003 212-674-8202
Fax 212-505-9526 Manufacturer Wholesale (Elementary School)
Ask for brochure. Products include Follow Your Nose (a game with 30 distinct aroma samples), Perfume Maker (chemically create more than 100 different fragrances), and many preschool wood puzzles of nature and science.

SMETHPORT SPECIALTY CO.
One Magnetic Avenue, Smethport, PA   16749   800-772-8697
814-887-5508   Fax 814-887-9272   Manufacturer   Wholesale
(Elementary School)
Ask for 32-page catalog. Science magnetic play sets, where magnetic
characters are placed on a scenic board, include Magnetic Dinosaurs,
Ocean Adventure, Magnetic Zoo, and Magnetic Adventure. Many other
products include educational games and puzzles.

TEDCO, INC.
Contact Jane Shadle 498 S Washington St, Hagerstown, IN 47346
800-654-6357 765-486-4527 Fax 765-489-5752
Email jane@tedcotoys.com   http://www.tedcotoys.com
Manufacturer Distributor   (Elementary School to Adult)
Ask for 10-page catalog. Toys include the TEDCO Gyroscope, games &
mazes, The Original Blocks and Marbles, Explorer Wrist Compass,
Magna-Trix, Rattleback, Right Angle Prisms, Solar Science Kit, and
more.

TESSELATIONS
688 W 1st St, Suite 5, Tempe, AZ 85281 800-655-5341 602-967-7455
Fax 602-967-7582   Email tessella@futureone.com
http://tesselations.com Manufacturer Wholesale Retail Mail Order
(Elementary School to Adult)
Ask for 8-page catalog. Puzzles that creatively combine math, art and
fun, including Monkey Business; Spin, Rock & Roll, a 3-D puzzle that
creates tops, pendulums, balls, and more; Tessel-Gons; Tessel-Gon Stars;
Tessellation Kaleidoscope; Tangrams; Captured Worlds, panoramic
projections on polyhedra; and many more. Classroom kits available.

TRIGRAM S. A.

8a puits-godet, CH-2000 Neuchatel, Switzerland 41-32-721-28-38
Fax 41-32-721-28-46 Email info@trigam.ch http://www.trigam.ch
Manufacturer Wholesale (All Ages)
Ask for brochure. 3-D puzzles and games based on mathematical theories. Products include Pentagor, Trigam Circus, Trigam 2, Zodiacube, DRHOMBX, Magic Diamond, Geometric Pearls, Twin Golden Diamond, and Trigam X.

UNIVERSITY GAMES CORP.

1633 Adrian Road, Burlingame, CA 94101 650-692-2500
Fax 650-692-2770 Manufacturer (Elementary School)
Ask for catalog. Toys available include Great Explorations, Raintree Puzzles, SlideMaster, The World's Greatest Paint Set, and more.

VECTA BLOCKS INC.

Contact Scott Jones 1515 Pitfield, St. Laurent, Quebec, Canada H4S
1G3 514-956-9300 Email vecta@openface.ca Manufacturer
(Elementary School to High School)
Vecta blocks are unique building blocks manufactured with Aerospace technology. They can be used to construct very precise, three-dimensional geometric figures such as the Archimedian polyhedra and even more complex polyhedra. These blocks can build "Buckeyball" on several scales of size, also known as the carbon-60 molecule. They can also build regular structures such as geodesic domes, helicopters and unlimited creative structures.

WIT CRAFTS
50 Main St, Malden, MA   02148
781-324-0114   Fax 781-322-7208
Email jqshan@aol.com
Manufacturer Wholesale (All Ages)
Ask for brochure.   Hand-made,
mahogany-wood novelty items that are
both   inspiring   art   and   witty
entertainment. Science items include
Rolling Balls, Jigsaw Puzzles, Trees
with Birds and Monkeys, Animals Set,
Dinosaurs Set, Gears & Dial, and more.

Clock Kit
Photo Courtesy of Wit Crafts

Y AND B ASSOCIATES
33 Primrose Lane, Hempstead, New
York 11550   516-481-0256
Fax 516-481-0256   Manufacturer
(Elementary   School   to   Middle
School)
Manufacturer of Archi-Forms (a model
and construction kit for the exploration
of physical space), Newton's Run (25
feet of tubing for flexible marble runs),
and Puzzabilities (create your own
optical illusions).

Archi-Forms Kit
Photo Courtesy of Y and B Associates

Chapter

10

Science Kits

Alex® Science Kits
Photo Courtesy of Alex/Panline USA

ALEX/PANLINE USA, INC.
454 South Dean St, Englewood, NJ
07631   800-666-ALEX
Fax 201-569-7944   Manufacturer
Wholesale (Elementary School)
Products include science kits, Luminous
Light, Eye Wonders, Marvelous
Magnets, The Air Up There, Water
Wonders, and Colorful Illusions.

ANDY VODA OPTICAL TOYS

RR 5, #387, Brattleboro, VT 05301 Tel/Fax 802-254-6115
Email avoda@together.net
http://www.together.net/~avoda/optical.htm/
Manufacturer Retail (All ages)
Ask for brochure. Phenakistascope with six magic wheels, Thaumatrope, Couples spinning pictures, Flipbooks, Greeting Flipbooks, Make-it-yourself Zoetrope.

BEAR CREEK TOYS, INC.

P O Box 247, Woodinville, WA 98072 800-232-7275 425-788-8104
Fax 425-844-2262 Manufacturer Wholesale (Elementary School)
Ask for 8-page catalog. Science and Nature Products include Critter Catcher Gift Set, Nature Net, Activity Jar, Bones & Rocks Earth Science Kit, Treasure Adventure, Plant Patch Growing Kits, Plant Patch Shovel, and more.

CHAOS

10920 Schuetz Road, Suite 1, St. Louis, MO   63146-5799
888-944-0129 314-567-9097 Fax 314-567-9123 Manufacturer Retail
mail order (Elementary School to High School)
Ask for brochure. Chaos, World of Motion, is a construction toy where an elevated marble falls though endless possible energy conversions created by the child or student. Award winning toy.

COPERNICUS

Contact Harris Tobias 100 E Main Street, Charlottesville, VA 22902
800-424-3950 804-296-6800 Fax 804-296-2154
Email Copernicus@1q.com   http://www.1q.com/Copernicus
Distributor   Wholesale   Retail Mail Order on Web Site
(Elementary School to Adult)
Ask for 12-page wholesale catalog. Member of Museum Store Association. Geodome, Volcano, Starglow, Rootbeer Kit, Bubblegum Kit, boomerangs, fly back plane, balloon car, Make a Clock Kit, Rattle Back, large Swinging Wonder, Echo Mike, Radiometer, Drinking Bird, Tornado Tube, magnifying glasses, astronaut ice cream, hand boiler, Magic Garden, abacus, Large Dome Making Kit, glow paint, glow bugs, spiral timer, auto compass, luminous star finder, swinging wonders.

Kitchen Chemistry
Photo Courtesy of
Creativity for Kids

CREATIVITY FOR KIDS

1802 Central Ave, Cleveland, OH 44115   800-642-2288   216-589-4800 Fax   216-589-4803   Email cservice@creativityforkids.com http://www.creativityforkids.com **Manufacturer Wholesale (Preschool and Elementary School)** Ask for 36-page catalog. Hands On Science kits, Kitchen Chemistry kit, Kitchen Botany, Creativity on Wheels, Beginning Birding, Spider Science, Busy with Bugs, Wee Enchanted Garden, Martian Garden, Sand Bag Buddy series.

CURIOSITY KITS

P O Box 811, Hunt Valley, MD
21031   800-584-KITS
410-584-2605   Fax 410-584-1247
Email ckitsinc@aol.com
Manufacturer Retail Mail Order
(Elementary School)
Ask for 28-page Kids Can Catalog.
Explore the adventures in science with
these Curiosity Kits: Bouncing Zoom
Balls, Super Dooper Bouncing Zoom
Balls, Kaleidoscope, National
Geographic/Curiosity Kits: Solar
System Puzzle and Coral Reef
Window Aquarium, Natural Soap Making, Vision Collision,
Glow-in-the-Dark Human Skeleton, and many more.

National Geographic Mola Pillow
Photo Courtesy of Curiosity Kits

CURIOUS DISCOVERIES, INC.

7911 Windspray Drive, Summerfield, NC   27358 800-585-2386
910-643-0432   Fax 910-643-0438   http://www.curiouskids.com
Manufacturer Wholesale (Elementary School)
Science discovery kits, nature products, animal replicas, and much more.

DELTA EDUCATION, INC.

P O Box 3000, Nashua, NH 03061-3000 800-442-5444
Fax 800-282-9560   603-886-4632   http://www.delta-ed.com
Manufacturer Retail Mail Order (Elementary School)
Ask for 60-page Hands-On Science catalog. This catalog is filled with
science kits, toys and educational materials. Also ask for information
about Delta Science Modules, SCIS3, and ESS. These three hands-on
programs are available through Delta Education.

EARTH LORE LTD.
94 Durand Road, Winnipeg, MB R2J 3T2, Canada 800-440-2630
204-654-1030   Fax 204-654-1018   http://www.earthlore.mb.ca
Manufacturer Wholesale (Elementary School)
Ask for brochure. Manufacturer of I Dig Dinosaurs, excavation kits where dinosaur models are hidden in a sand enclosure.

EDC PUBLISHING
10302 E 55th Place #B, Tulsa, OK 74146-6515 / P O Box 470663, Tulsa, OK 74146-6515   800-475-4522   918-622-4522
Fax 918-655-7919 http://www.edcpub.com   **Manufacturer Wholesale (Elementary School)**
Ask for Usborne Books catalog. Kids Kits contain a book and specially selected age-appropriate materials. Kids Kits include science products: Dinosaurs, Nature, At the Seaside, Dinosaurs Picture History, Science with Air, Things that Fly, Science with Magnets, Paper Planes, Batteries & Magnets, Science Experiments, Young Naturalist, and more.

EDMUND SCIENTIFIC COMPANY
101 E Gloucester Pike, Barrington, NJ 08007-1380 800-728-6999
609-573-3488 Fax 609-573-6272   http://www.edsci.com   **Retail (All ages)**
Ask for 112-page science reference catalog for educators. Since 1942 this well known scientific optical supplier also sells many other items including lasers, microscopes, camera/monitor systems, science classroom anatomy models, nature kits, laboratory safety equipment, balances, weather instruments, timers, magnets, small motors & pumps, robot kits, earth science kits, telescopes, museum animal replicas, and unique classroom materials for teachers.

EDUCATIONAL DESIGN, INC.
345 Hudson St, New York, NY 10014-4502 212-255-7900 800-221-9372 212-255-7900 Fax 212-675-6922 **Manufacturer Wholesale (Elementary School)**
Ask for 80-page catalog with complete line of educational materials including quality science labs and activity toys. Award winning toys include Electromagnetix, Slime Science, Home Planetarium, Solar System, Electronics and Volcanoes. Their catalog lists regional sales representatives.

Our Amazing Bridges Architecture Kit
Photo Courtesy of Educational Design

ELENCO ELECTRONICS
150 W Carpenter, Wheeling, IL 60090 800-533-2441 847-541-3800 Fax 847-520-0085
Email elenco@elenco.com
http://www.elenco.com
Manufacturer Retail Mail Order (Middle School to Adult)
Ask for catalog and brochure on Elenco Electronics Kits. Kits are designed for educational learning experiences for students and hobbyists. Many, but not all, of these kits require soldering.

Elenco Electronics Kits
Photo Courtesy of Elenco Electronics

EXPLORATORIUM STORE
3601 Lyon St, San Francisco, CA 94123   415-561-0393
http://www.exploratorium.edu   Retail Mail Order   (All ages)
See web page that is filled with quality science toys and books, including
the following toys: Megabubbles Kit, The Kaleidoscope Book and Kit,
Zoetrope, Wild Wood, Magnetron, Gyros, Curiosity Box, Eagle
Microscope, Mirage Maker, Micro-Bank, Erector Sets, Paradox 3-D
Jigsaw Puzzle, and Ellipto.

FRANCIS FAMILY TOYS LTD.
1314 Rufina Circle #A9, Santa Fe, NM 87505 505-473-4501
Fax 505-473-4519 Manufacturer Wholesale (Elementary School)
Ask for brochure. Manufacturer of CREATEures, stuffed cotton animals
that you paint. Also, heirloom quality folk toys including Jacob's Ladder,
Tie Dye Kit, and preschool wooden toys.

FRANK SCHAFFER PUBLICATIONS
23740 Hawthorne Blvd, Torrance, CA 90505 800-609-1735
Fax 800-837-7260 http://www.frankschaffer.com Manufacturer
(Preschool to Elementary School)
Ask for 44-page Judy Instructo catalog. Judi Instructo, a division of
Frank Schaffer Publications, offers Science Quest Kits on Earth, Weather,
Light & Color, Magnets, Dinosaurs & Fossils, Insects, and Sound.

FREUD, MORRIS & WILLIAMS
200 Fifth Ave, Suite 835, New York, NY 10010 Distributor
(Elementary School)
Ask for 15-page catalog. Distributor of Science Tech microscopes,
telescopes, binoculars, videoscope, anatomical models, magnets,
periscopes, chemistry lab kit, magnifier, bug viewer, stereoscope, and
more.

GALT AMERICA
Distributor of GALT Toys, 230
Woodmont Road, Milford, CT
06460 800-899-4258
Fax 203-876-2739
http://www.galt-co.uk
Distributor Wholesale
(Preschool to Elementary School)
Ask for 56-page catalog. These
well-known toys are Made-in-United
Kingdom. Science toys include
Seasonal Puzzles, Water Puzzles,
Marble Run, Magnet Building,
Connecta-Straws, Young Explorer

Growing Things Kit
Photo Courtesy of Galt America

series, Telescope, Microscope, Binoculars, Crystal Radio Kit, Intruder
Alarm Kit, Electrical Games Kit, Bug Watch Kit, Ecology Kit, and more.

HOMECRAFTERS MANUFACTURING
1859 Kenion Point, Snellville, GA 30078 770-985-5460
Fax 770-978-3012   Email hmctoys@aol.com
http://homecrafters-mfg.com Manufacturer Wholesale and Retail
(Elementary School)
Ask for brochure describing "I Made My...Periscope!" kit and "I Made
My...Kaleidoscope!" kit and other Home Crafted Toys.

HUNTAR CO. INC.
Contact Tammy Lawrence 473 Littlefield Ave, So. San Francisco,
CA 94080 800-566-8686 650-873-8282 Fax 650-873-8292
Email Huntar.Magnet@worldnet.att.net Manufacturer Wholesale
(Elementary School to High School)
Ask for 24-page catalog. Magnetic products include activity kits, wands,
marbles, chips, shaped magnets, puzzle wheels, math & letter wheels,
play boards, and floating rings.

IDEAL SCHOOL SUPPLY COMPANY
11000 S Lavergne Ave, Oak Lawn, IL 60453 800-845-8149
http://www.ifair.com Distributor Retail Mail Order
(Preschool to Elementary School)
Ask for the 50-page teacher catalog. Science measurement materials,
chemistry experiment beakers and test tubes, equilateral prisms, physics
pulleys, thermometers, classroom science kits, magnetic toys, natural
science materials.

INSECT LORE
P O Box 1535, Shafter, CA 93263 800-LIVE-BUG 805-746-6047
Fax 805-746-0334   Email insect@lightspeed.net
http://www.insectlore.com   Manufacturer Wholesale
Retail Mail Order (Elementary School)
Ask for 32-page catalog. Distributor of many science kits and books on
nature's creatures, including ant farms, butterflies, insects, plants & trees,
science project ideas, frogs and amphibians, and nature videos.

K & M INTERNATIONAL
1955 Midway Drive, Twinsburg, OH 44087 800-800-9678
216-963-8678   Fax 216-425-3777   Manufacturer   Wholesale
(Elementary School to Adult)
Anatomically accurate stuffed and molded animals creatures of nature. Stuffed products include National Geographic WildLife Legends, AZA Animals, Maddalena Series, African Animals, Rainforest Animals, Animals of the World, North American Animals, Aquatic Animals, puppets, and more. Molded products include containers of small, hand-held animal toys and numerous varieties of kits, puzzles, stickers, and more.

K'NEX INDUSTRIES, INC
Education Division, 2990 Bergey Road, P O Box 700, Hatfield, PA 19440 800-543-5639 215-997-7722 Fax 215-996-4222
Email knex@provicenet.com http://www.knex.com Manufacturer
(Elementary School to High School)
A unique, educational construction toy. Science educational products include Classroom Super Set & Educator Guide, Solar System Set, Simple Machines Sets.

KRISTAL EDUCATIONAL INC.
Distributed by Ira Cooper, Inc., P O Box 2137, Woodinville, WA 98072 206-720-6264   Fax 206-720-6317
http://www.mysteriousart.com   Distributor Wholesale
(Elementary School to High School)
Ask for 26-page catalog. Mineral crystal growing kits, including Space Age Crystal Kits; Crystal Spheres, Pyramids & Jewelry; Crystal Caves; Dab'a'Dino (Paintable stuffed dinosaurs); National Geographic Society's Expedition Series; Gem Tree Kits; Archeology Kits; and more.

LAWRENCE HALL OF SCIENCE
University of California, Berkeley, CA 94720-5200 510-642-1016
Fax 510-642-1055   Email lhsstore@uclink4.berkeley.edu
http://www.lhs.berkeley.edu (All Ages)
See web site filled with books, teachers' and parents' guides, science kits, videos, and ordering instructions. Known as Eureka!: Teaching Tools from the Lawrence Hall of Science.

LEARNING RESOURCES, INC.
Contact Lisa Hoffmann   380 N Fairway Drive, Vernon Hills, IL
60061   800-222-3909   847-573-8400   Fax 847-573-8425
http://www.learningresources.com   Manufacturer Wholesale
(Preschool and Elementary School)
Exceptional range of award-winning educational toys. Ask for 72-page catalog. Pretend & Play Calculator Cash Register, math and science measurement materials, geometry shapes, base ten products, thermometers, Power of Science line of science accessories, Idea Factory Science Kits, the Investigator Slide Viewer with slide strip sets, the Quantum Big Screen Microscope.

LEGO DACTA - THE EDUCATIONAL DIVISION OF LEGO SYSTEMS, INC.
555 Taylor Rd, P O Box 1600, Enfield, CN 06083-1600 800-527-8339
Manufacturer   Retail and Wholesale   Distributed by PITSCO
800-362-4308 (Elementary School to High School)
Gear, lever and pulley toys, Technic classroom kits, Technic control centers, teacher's guide books, Pneumatics, Logowriter Robotics for Apple and MS-DOS, Control Lab for Apple and MS-DOS.

THE MAGNET SOURCE
Master Magnetics, Inc., 607 Gilbert St, Castle Rock, CO 80104
800-874-6248 303-688-3966 Fax 303-688-5303
Email magsales@magnetsource.com http://www.magnetsource.com
Manufacturer Wholesale (Elementary School to Adult)
Ask for catalog. Magnetic kits, toys, and educational products, including
magnetic balls, wands, Discovery Kits, Earth globes, tape, and more.

MAST DISTRIBUTION INC.
Distributor of LASY Toys, 54 Ballymore Drive, Aurora, Ontario
L4G 7E6, Canada 888-553-6278 905-727-2985 Fax 905-727-3933
Email dnniesin@netrover.com http://www.lasy.com Distributor
Wholesale (Elementary School)
Ask for 24-page LASY Didact (Educational) catalog. LASY is a quality,
Made-in-Germany, construction toy. Many educational, scientific, and
technology-oriented toys are available.

MAYFLOWER DEVELOPMENT AND TRADING CORP.
P O Box 705, Bellevue, WA 98009
425-747-7766   Fax 425-957-9384
Email switchon@concentric.net
http://www.concentric.net/~switchon
Manufacturer Wholesale Retail
Mail Order
(Elementary School to High School)
Manufacturer of Switch On!:
Innovative Electronic Building Blocks.
Have fun setting up easy-to-connect,
safe circuit blocks to switch on: a light

Switch On!
Photo Courtesy of
Mayflower Development

bulb, a fire engine, a flashing door bell, an electric fan, or create your own
circuit. An excellent, fun way to teach electrical circuits to children.

MIDWEST MODEL SUPPLY CO.

12040 S Aero Dr, Plainfield, IL 60544   800-573-7029 815-254-2151
Fax 815-254-2445   Email mwmodelsup@aol.com   Distributor
Wholesale   Quantity School Orders   (All Ages)
Ask for literature.   Source for Estes Rockets & accessories, bridge
building kits, aero-space models, plane programs, mousetrap racers, and
model making materials.

MORE BALLS THAN MOST

Contact Virginia Wages-Plotkin 26 W 17th St, # 702, New York, NY
10011 800-544-3688, ext 13 212-691-9660, ext 13 Fax 212-691-9633
Email Virginia@MBTMNY.mhs.compuserve.com   Manufacturer
Distributor Wholesale (Elementary School to Adult)
Ask for 20-page catalog. Toys include hot air balloon kits, The Rokit
(launch a soda bottle up to 50 feet with compressed air), Buster
Bloodvessel (wooden and wire puzzles), Optical (pocket optical illusion
jigsaw), Penultimate (a pen that floats on air and spins on a frictionless
bed), juggling supplies, and more.

NATIONAL ENERGY FOUNDATION

Contact Gary Swan 5225 Wiley Post Way, Suite 170, Salt Lake City,
UT 84116 801-539-1406 Fax 801-539-1451 Email info@nef1.org
http://www.nef1.org (Elementary School to High School)
This nonprofit organization provides programs and materials to help
promote an awareness of energy-related issues. Ask for 15-page catalog
of publications and science kits. Materials include Out of the Rock, a
mineral resource and mining education program for K-8 produced in
conjunction with the U. S. Bureau of Mines.

NATURE'S TOYLAND

Subsidiary of Penn-Plax, Inc., 720 Stewart Ave, Garden City, NY 11530 516-222-1020 Manufacturer Wholesale (Elementary School to Adult)

This manufacturer of pet care products makes educational kits, including Tweety-Your First Bird Cage Kit, Tom and Jerry Hamster/Gerbil Home, The Little Mermaid Goldfish Aquarium and Collection Tank, The Little Mermaid Hermit Crab World, Ninja Turtles Collection Play Tank, Tweety-My First Bird Watching Kit, Bugs Bunny Rabbit/Guinea Pig Cage and Small Animal Habitats for hamsters and gerbils. See your local pet care retail store.

OWI INCORPORATED

Contact Craig Morioka 1160 Mahalo Place, Compton, CA 90220-5443 310-638-4732 Fax 310-638-8347 Email owi@ix.netcom.com http://www.owirobot.com Manufacturer Wholesale (Nine Years to Adult)

Ask for brochure on Robotics and for information on retail distributors. This manufacturer makes several different robotic kits requiring different levels of assembly sophistication. The new

OWI Solar Car
Photo Courtesy of OWI

Triple Action Solar Car Kit allows batteries or solar power with a multi-speed transmission.

**Scientific Explorer
Nature Adventures**
Photo Courtesy of Scientific Explorer

SCIENTIFIC EXPLORER, INC.
4020 E Madison, Suite 326, Seattle,
WA 98112 800-900-1182
206-322-7611 Fax 206-322-7610
Email sciex@scientificexplorer.com
http://www.scientificexplorer.com
http://www.gettoys.com
Manufacturer Retail Mail Order
(Elementary School to Adult)
Ask for 16-page catalog. Manufacturer
of science and adventure kits including
Fun with Your Cat, Fun with Your
Dog, Smithsonian Adventures Series,
Aerial Camera, High Altitude Launcher,
Science of Scent, Make Animal Soaps, Kitchen Science, Educational
Cooking Center, Nature Adventures, Exploring Electronics, Science of
Sound, and many more.

SMALL WORLD TOYS
5711 Buckingham Parkway, Culver City, CA 90230 800-421-4153
310-645-9680 Fax 310-410-9606 Manufacturer Distributor
Wholesale (Preschool and Elementary School)
Gyroscopes, Gravity Graph, inflatable globes, Backyard Scientist, mineral
sets, Bug World, dinosaur skeleton kits, Polyopticon optical toy kits, Bug
Hotel, magnetic toys, Gigantic Glow Stars, dinosaur models, origami kits,
Whirlybirds, Newton's Yo-Yo, Finger Tops, Astronaut Food, animal sets,
magnifier toys, Sparkling Wheels, Relaxable Globe Balls.

SOMERVILLE HOUSE

3080 Yonge St, Suite 5000, Toronto, Ontario, Canada M4N 3N1
800-387-9776 Fax 800-260-9777 416-488-5938 Fax 416-488-5506
Email sombooks@goodmedia.com   http://www.sombooks.com
Manufacturer Distributor Wholesale (Elementary School)
Ask for 32-page catalog. The Bones Book with plastic skeleton, dinosaur books with plastic skeletons, The Environmental Detective Kit. Books packaged with toy models. Also The Bug Book & Bottle, The Ultimate Science Kit, Snail Tongues and Spider Fangs, Bug Eyes and Butterfly Wings, Coral Reef, Birds of Prey, Insects and Spiders, Snakes and Lizards, and more.

SUN-MATE CORP.

8223 Remmet Ave, Canoga Park, CA 91304 818-883-7766
Fax 818-883-8171   http://www.sun-mate.com   Manufacturer
Wholesale (Elementary School)
Science educational solar toys, wooden motor kits, adventure kits, and more.

TEDCO, INC.

Contact Jane Shadle   498 S Washington St, Hagerstown, IN 47346 800-654-6357 765-486-4527 Fax 765-489-5752
Email jane@tedcotoys.com
http://www.tedcotoys.com
Manufacturer Distributor (Elementary School to Adult)
Ask for 10-page catalog. Toys include the TEDCO Gyroscope, games & mazes, The Original Blocks and Marbles, Explorer Wrist Compass, Magna-Trix, Rattleback, Right Angle Prisms, Solar Science Kit, and more.

Blocks and Marbles™
Photo Courtesy of TEDCO

TREE OF KNOWLEDGE
Contact Henry Bunzl, Managing Director   Yasur, D. N. Misgav 20150, Israel   972-4-9960320   Fax 972-4-9969244   Manufacturer Distributor (Elementary School to High School)
Ask for brochure. Manufacturer of Scientific Experiment Kits.

TWC OF AMERICA, INC.
Contact Terry Weber   9663 Hwy 144 North, Kewaskum, WI 53040 800-301-7592   414-692-6835   Fax 414-692-6709
http://www.twcoa.com   http://www.tweber.com   Manufacturer Wholesale (Elementary School to Adult)
Ask for 8-page TWC Gifts Catalog, including quality products for nature lovers: Insect & Pond Nets, various wooden Nature Houses, bat houses, OBE II Bird Feeder, Colonial Birdhouse Kits. Ask for 8-page Tweber Backyard Explorer Gear Catalog, including products for the young nature lover: Play Tent, Nature Houses, Nature Exploring & Catch-All Nets, Butterfly Loft, Leaf Press, Bird Houses, and Bird Feeders.

UNCLE MILTON INDUSTRIES, INC.
5717 Corsa Ave, Westlake Village, CA   91362-4001 800-869-7555 818-707-0800   Fax 818-707-0878   Email   antfarm@ix.netcom.com http://www.unclemilton.com   Manufacturer   Wholesale (Elementary School)
Seven-page catalog contains Ant Farms (Milton Levine invented the Ant Farm in 1956), Pocket Museums, Fossil Hunt, Krazy Klowns, Light-Up Critter City, BugJug, Star Theater home planetarium, Super GeoScope microscope, Hydro Greenhouse, Rock & Mineral Hunt, Surf Frogs. Surf Frogs is a live frog habitat where frogs grow from tadpoles.

THE WILD GOOSE COMPANY
375 Whitney Ave, 375 W 1455 S,
Salt Lake City, UT 84115
800-373-1498   801-466-1172
Fax 801-466-1186
http://www.widgoosescience.com
**Distributor Manufacturer Retail
Mail Order (Elementary School)**
Ask for 16-page catalog. Science
materials include Newton's Apple
Kits, Teacher Books, Megalab kits,
T-Shirts,   Posters,   Professional
Development   Training,   and
Student-Centered Programs.

**Newton's Apple®
Newton on Slime**
Photo Courtesy of
Wild Goose Company

Chapter

11 | Toys that Teach Science

ACTION PRODUCTS INT'L, INC.
344 Cypress Road, Ocala, FL 34472 800-772-2846 352-687-2202
Fax 352-687-4961   Email sales@apii.com   http://www.apii.com
Manufacturer Distributor Wholesale (Elementary School)
Educational toys about science, Woodkits (Prehistoric and Animals from
nature), Space Replicas, Imagninetics, Science in Action, and much more.

ALEX/PANLINE USA, INC.
454 South Dean St, Englewood, NJ 07631 800-666-ALEX
Fax 201-569-7944 **Manufacturer Wholesale (Elementary School)**
Products include science kits, Luminous Light, Eye Wonders,
Marvelous Magnets, The Air Up There, Water Wonders, and Colorful
Illusions.

ALL MAGNETICS INC.

930-C S Placentia Ave, Placentia, CA 92670 714-632-1754
Fax 714-632-1757 Manufacturer Distributor
(Elementary School to High School)
Ask for brochure. Manufacturer of the Levi-top Earth activity set.

ALPI INTERNATIONAL LTD.

P O Box 8835, Emeryville, CA
94662 800-678-ALPI 510-655-6456
Fax 510-655-2093
http://www.alpi.net Manufacturer
Wholesale
(Preschool to Elementary School)
Ask for 38-page catalog. Squeezable
preschool toys including famous
characters, animals of all varieties,
dinosaurs, and more. Also, Glow in
the Dark chalk, paint, and toys. Many
science toys including Star Finder,
Optic Wonder, gyroscopes, and more.

Star Finder™ Kit
Photo Courtesy of ALPI Intn'l

AMERICAN PAPER OPTICS

Contact Andrew Balogh 3080 Bartlett Corporate Drive, Bartlett, TN
38133   800-767-8429   901-381-1515   Fax 901-381-1517   Email
abalogh@lunaweb.net Manufacturer Wholesale Retail Mail Order
(Elementary School to Adult)
Manufacturer of Holiday Specs, paper eye glasses that create images
around small bright white holiday lights.

**Anatex™
Shape 'n' Color Coaster**
Photo Courtesy of Anatex Enterprises

ANATEX ENTERPRISES
15929 Arminta St, Van Nuys, CA 91406   800-999-9599   818-908-1888 Fax 818-908-0656
Email   anatex@anatex.com
http://www.anatex.com
Manufacturer   Distributor
(Preschool to Primary)
Ask for 24-page catalog. Quality toys for preschoolers that encourage the development of both cognitive and motor skills.   Products include Magnetic Bug Life Table, Ten Counter, Fleur Rollercoaster Table, Cyclone, Wonder Bug Mazes, Magnetooli, Pathfinder, Shape 'n' Color Coaster, and more.

ANDY VODA OPTICAL TOYS
RR 5, #387, Brattleboro, VT 05301 Tel/Fax 802-254-6115
Email avoda@together.net
http://www.together.net/~avoda/optical.htm/ Manufacturer Retail
(All ages)
Ask for brochure. Phenakistascope with six magic wheels, Thaumatrope, Couples spinning pictures, Flipbooks, Greeting Flipbooks, Make-it-yourself Zoetrope.

ARCHIE MC PHEE
P O Box 30852, Seattle, WA 98103 206-745-0711 Fax 425-745-7143
Email mcphee@mcphee.com   http://www.halcyon.com/mcphee/
Retail Mail Order Retail store located at 3510 Stone Way N, Seatle,
WA 206-545-8344 (All ages)
Ask for 15-page catalog. Fun, inexpensive toys and novelties. Insects,
bats, turtles, fish, dinosaurs, eye balls, beanie with propeller, iguanas,
wall walker octopus.

ARK FOUNDATION
34 Smith St, Norwalk, CN 06851 888-ARK-8500 914-421-2195
Fax 203-855-7660 http://www.arkfoundation.com Manufacturer
Retail Mail Order (Elementary School to High School)
Manufacturer of Preservation Puzzles, large and colorful foam puzzles of
rare, exotic and often endangered species.

BATTAT INC.
44 Martina Circle, P O Box 1264, Plattsburgh, NY   12901
800-247-6144   518-562-2200   Fax 518-562-2203
http://www.battat-toys.com   Montreal, Canada 514-341-6000
Manufacturer Wholesale (Elementary School)
Manufacturer of Two Way Microscope.

BENJAMIN INTERNATIONAL

Contact Lynn Dimon   139 Bacon Pond, Woodbury, CT   06798
800-488-4699   Fax 888-488-4699   Email LDimon@aol.com
Manufacturer Distributor Wholesale (Elementary School to Adult)
Ask for 24-page catalog. Manufacturer and distributor of novelty items
including Glow-in-the-Dark Stars and Planets, Tornado Tube, Collectable
Tin Toy Animals, Sand Pets, LaserSpin, Hologram Glasses, Aero-Prop,
Hand Boiler, Drinking Bird, Kritterscopes, Lotus Puzzle, Blacklites,
Electronic Laser Ball, and Strobe Light.

The Teaching Tank™
Photo Courtesy of Captivation

CAPTIVATION, INC.

101 Connecticut Ave, Nashua, NH
03060-5129 603-889-1156
Fax 603-880-5334
Email capinc@tchg.com
http://www.tchg.com **Manufacturer
Distributor   Retail Mail Order
(Elementary School to High School)**
Ask for brochure. Manufacturer of The
Teaching Tank, a see-through system
that provides opportunity for numerous
visual experiments in most science
subjects, including experiments on
acids, color, density and solubility, dew
point, diffusion, volcanic action, centripetal force, horticulture, and many
more. Use The Teaching Tank Discovery Book, Volumes 1 and 2, for
experiment descriptions, each over 100 pages.

CARLISLE CO.
P O Box 21029, Carson City, NV 89721 800-233-3931
Fax 800-245-3306 Manufacturer Distributor Retail Mail Order (Elementary School to Adult)
Ask for 24-page catalog. Novelties from science and nature including Holographic Wands, Mobiles, Anti-Gravity Revolution, Lightning Balls, Kinetic Chaos pendulum, Kinetic Sealife, Perpetual Motion Wheels, Solar System motion space sculpture, Rave Wave dual-colored waves, Spiral Timer, and much, much more.

Balance Balls
Photo Courtesy of Carlisle Co.

CARSON & COPITAR
Contact Jeni Sikorski 200 E Second St, Unit 5, Huntington Station, NY 11746 800-967-8427 516-427-6570 Fax 516-427-6749
Email jsikorski@carson-optical.com   http://carson-optical.com
Manufacturer (Elementary School to Adult)
Ask for brochures. Manufacturer of binoculars, magnifiers, telescopes, and a wide variety of quality optical instruments, including X-Scope, a multi-use optical pocket tool.

CELESTRON INTERNATIONAL
Contact Linda Waible 2835 Columbia St, Torrance, CA 90503
310-328-9560 Fax 310-212-5835 Email l_waible@celestron.com
http://www.celestron.com Manufacturer Distributor (High School
to Adult)
Ask for catalogs: Telescopes for Astronomy, Celestron Telescopes,
Celestron Binoculars & Spotting Scopes, Lab Grade Microscopes, and
Celestron Accessories. Major manufacturer of telescopes.

CHAOS
10920 Schuetz Road, Suite 1, St. Louis, MO   63146-5799
888-944-0129 314-567-9097 Fax 314-567-9123 Manufacturer Retail
mail order (Elementary School to High School)
Ask for brochure. Chaos, World of Motion, is a construction toy where
an elevated marble falls though endless possible energy conversions
created by the child or student. Award winning toy.

CHILD'S PLAY
Contact Joe Gardner   67 Minot Ave, Auburn, ME   04210
800-472-0099 Fax 800-854-6989 973-731-3777 Fax 973-731-3740
cplay@mail.idt.net Manufacturer (Preschool to Elementary School)
Ask for 24-page catalog. Books, toys and games include Time Tunnel,
Bats, Spiders, Children of the Sun (Astronomy), Metamorphoses
(Butterflies and Frogs), Sorting and Matching, Shape and Color,
Arithmetic Games, and more.

CHILDCRAFT EDUCATION CORP.

20 Kilmer Road, P. O. Box 3081, Edison, NJ 08818-3081 800-631-5652 Distributor Retail http://childcraft.com (Preschool to Elementary School)

Ask for the 200-page catalog. Math toys, aquariums, plant growing kit, seashells, root garden, ant farm, microscope, optical toys, magnetic toys, weather materials, globes. Educational materials.

CHILDWOOD

Contact Karen Beierle 8873 Woodbank Dr, Bainbridge Island, WA 98110 800-362-9825 206-842-9290 Fax 206-842-5107 Email childwood@aol.com Manufacturer Retail Mail Order (Preschool and Elementary School)

Ask for 14-page catalog. Six science themes are packaged with sturdy, full-color, wooden magnetic figures. All hands-on science sets include stories, activities and reproducible mini-books. Sets include Life Cycles: The Butterfly, The Hen and The Frog; The Farm; Sealife; The Bear Cave; Dinosaurs; and Weather.

Wooden Magnetic Figures
Photo Courtesy of Childwood

CLUB EARTH

A division of Easy Aces, Inc. 30 Martin St, Suite 381, Cumberland, RI 02864 800-327-8415 401-333-3090 Fax 401-333-3123 Distributor Wholesale (All Ages)

Ask for brochure. Toys, puppets, and novelties related to animals and living creatures of the Earth.

COPERNICUS
Contact Harris Tobias 100 E Main Street, Charlottesville, VA 22902
800-424-3950 804-296-6800 Fax 804-296-2154
Email Copernicus@1q.com   http://www.1q.com/Copernicus
Distributor Wholesale Retail Mail Order on Web Site
(Elementary School to Adult)
Ask for 12-page wholesale catalog. Member of Museum Store Association. Geodome, Volcano, Starglow, Rootbeer Kit, Bubblegum Kit, boomerangs, fly back plane, balloon car, Make a Clock Kit, Rattle Back, large Swinging Wonder, Echo Mike, Radiometer, Drinking Bird, Tornado Tube, magnifying glasses, astronaut ice cream, hand boiler, Magic Garden, abacus, Large Dome Making Kit, glow paint, glow bugs, spiral timer, auto compass, luminous star finder, swinging wonders.

CREATIVE PUBLICATIONS
5040 W 111th St, Oak Lawn, IL 60453-5008 800-624-0822 Email creativepublications@tribune.com Retail (Elementary School)
Ask for the 115-page catalog filled with educational materials for math, geometry, science, science measurement, and educational curricula. Also science posters.

CREATIVITY FOR KIDS
1802 Central Ave, Cleveland, OH 44115 800-642-2288 216-589-4800
Fax 216-589-4803   Email cservice@creativityforkids.com
http://www.creativityforkids.com   Manufacturer Wholesale
(Preschool and Elementary School)
Ask for 36-page catalog. Hands On Science kits, Kitchen Chemistry kit, Kitchen Botany, Creativity on Wheels, Beginning Birding, Spider Science, Busy with Bugs, Wee Enchanted Garden, Martian Garden, Sand Bag Buddy series.

CUISENAIRE - DALE SEYMOUR PUBLICATIONS
10 Bank St, P O Box 5026, White Plains, NY 10602-5026
800-237-0338   Email info@awl.com   http://cuisenaire.com
http://awl.com/dsp/ Distributor Retail (Elementary School)
Major supplier of resources for the classroom and home learning
environment. The 224-page K-6 Catalog, 113-page Middle School
Catalog, and 112-page Secondary Math & Science Catalog includes math,
manipulatives, science, and teacher resources.

CURIOSITY KITS
P O Box 811, Hunt Valley, MD 21031 800-584-KITS 410-584-2605
Fax 410-584-1247 Email ckitsinc@aol.com Manufacturer Retail
Mail Order (Elementary School)
Ask for 28-page Kids Can Catalog. Explore the adventures in science
with these Curiosity Kits: Bouncing Zoom Balls, Super Dooper
Bouncing Zoom Balls, Kaleidoscope, National Geographic/Curiosity
Kits: Solar System Puzzle and Coral Reef Window Aquarium, Natural
Soap Making, Vision Collision, Glow-in-the-Dark Human Skeleton, and
many more.

CURIOUS DISCOVERIES, INC.
7911 Windspray Drive, Summerfield, NC 27358 800-585-2386
910-643-0432   Fax 910-643-0438   http://www.curiouskids.com
Manufacturer Wholesale (Elementary School)
Science discovery kits, nature products, animal replicas, and much more.

Great Gizmos Demo Kit
Photo Courtesy of Damert Company

DAMERT COMPANY
1609 4th Street, Berkeley, CA 94710
800-231-3722 510-524-7400
Fax 510-524-4466
Email damert@aol.com
h t t p : / / w w w . d a m e r t . c o m
Manufacturer Wholesale
(Elementary School to Adult)
Ask for 36-page catalog. Science toys include 3-D Slide Puzzles, Jungle Bungles puzzles, Concentra puzzle, Tiazzle Puzzles, Master Triazzles, coffee mugs, bulletin boards, many science mobiles, StarShines astronomy stickers, diffraction toys, Laser Top, Spiral Mobiles, Turbo Sparkler YoYo, liquid crystal toys and novelties, Little Critter Kaleidoscope, Butterflies of the World, bird feeder kit, Zoetrope, Vector Flexor, Echo Rocket, Spacephones, Tornado Tube, science charts and posters.

DAVIS LIQUID CRYSTALS INC.
15021 Wicks Blvd, San Leandro, CA 94577   800-677-5575
Fax 510-351-2328   Manufacturer Distributor Wholesale
(Elementary School to Adult)
Manufacturer of liquid crystal novelties that change color when touched. Products include SolarZone T-shirts with science designs that change from indoor black and white to outdoor full color.

DELTA EDUCATION, INC.

P O Box 3000, Nashua, NH 03061-3000   800-442-5444
Fax 800-282-9560   603-886-4632   http://www.delta-ed.com
Manufacturer Retail Mail Order (Elementary School)
Ask for 60-page Hands-On Science catalog. This catalog is filled with
science kits, toys and educational materials. Also ask for information
about Delta Science Modules, SCIS3, and ESS. These three hands-on
programs are available through Delta Education.

DEXTER EDUCATIONAL TOYS, INC.

P O Box 630861, Miami, FL 33163 305-931-7426 Fax 305-931-0552
Manufacturer Wholesale (Preschool to Elementary School)
Ask for brochure. Manufacturer of creative career role playing costumes
and puppets, including The Scientist, The Teacher, The Police Officer,
and many more. Ask about local distributor or purchase on school
letterhead.

DIDAX INC. EDUCATIONAL RESOURCES

Contact Martin Kennedy 395 Main
St, Rowley, MA 01969 800-458-0024
978-948-2340 Fax 978-948-2813
Email catalog@didaxinc.com
http://www.didaxinc.com   Retail
(Elementary School)
Ask for 128-page catalog of hands-on
materials   in   elementary   school
mathematics and science.

**Accordian-fold Books
on Endangered Animals**
Photo Courtesy of Didax Inc.

DIMENSIONS IN LEARNING, INC.

P O Box 639, Forest Park, IL 60130 888-366-6628 708-366-6117 Fax 708-366-8348   Email nkokat@sprintmail.com   Distributor (Elementary School to High School)

Ask for 24-page catalog. Distributor of Valiant Technology Ltd. educational materials from Great Britain. Products include Roamer, robot that teaches mathematics; Inventa, system of invention and design; Tronix, system of science and technology using electronics; and more.

The Wizzzer® Gyroscope
Photo Courtesy of Duncan Toy

DUNCAN TOY CO.

15981 Valplast Rd, Middlefield, OH 44062   800-356-8396 440-632-1631 Fax 440-632-1581 http://www.flamprod.com Manufacturer Distributor (All Ages) Manufacturer of Duncan Yo-Yo's. Ask for brochure and Teacher's Guide: Teaching Science with the Yo-Yo.

EBERHARD, VON HUENE & ASSOCIATES

346, rue Aime Vincent, Vaudreuil, Quebec, Canada   J7V 5V5
514-424-0186   Fax 514-455-5126   Email eberhard@globale.net
Manufacturer (Elementary School to Adult)
Ask for brochure. Manufacturer of Sound Bytes, the verbal game in
which a player's recorded verbal statements are "sliced 'n diced" when
replayed so that the information can be recovered and understood by
another player. Fun potential for classroom student play on academic
topics.

ECO-BRAZIL CORP.

**Contact Elizabeth Howitt 250 West
94th Street, #13J, New York, NY
10025 800-272-3811 212-222-1285
Fax 212-222-1154   Manufacturer
Wholesale Retail
(Elementary School)**
Ask for brochure. Manufacturer of
soft, colorful Moving Masks: Shark,
Elephant, Frog, Bird, Alligator, Wolf,
Lion, Dragon, Monkey, and Rabbit.
Also soft, colorful Funny Bugs
puppets: Grasshopper, Spider, Bee,

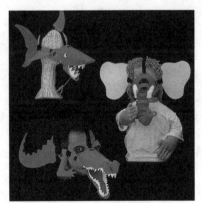

Moving Masks™
Photo Courtesy of Eco-Brazil

and Lady Bug. As well as Mobiles, small Hand Puppets, and Finger
Puppets.

EDMUND SCIENTIFIC COMPANY
101 E Gloucester Pike, Barrington, NJ 08007-1380 800-728-6999 609-573-3488 Fax 609-573-6272 http://www.edsci.com Retail (All ages)
Ask for 112-page science reference catalog for educators. Since 1942 this well known scientific optical supplier also sells many other items including lasers, microscopes, camera/monitor systems, science classroom anatomy models, nature kits, laboratory safety equipment, balances, weather instruments, timers, magnets, small motors & pumps, robot kits, earth science kits, telescopes, museum animal replicas, and unique classroom materials for teachers.

EDUCATIONAL DESIGN, INC.
345 Hudson St, New York, NY 10014-4502   212-255-7900 800-221-9372   212-255-7900   Fax 212-675-6922   Manufacturer Wholesale (Elementary School)
Ask for 80-page catalog with complete line of educational materials including quality science labs and activity toys. Award winning toys include Electromagnetix, Slime Science, Home Planetarium, Solar System, Electronics and Volcanoes. Catalog lists regional sales representatives.

EDUCATIONAL INSIGHTS
Contact Customer Service Department 16941 Keegan Ave, Carson, CA 90746 800-995-4436 310-884-2000 Fax 800-995-0506 Email service@edin.com http://www.edin.com Manufacturer Retail and Wholesale (Elementary School)
Ask for 32-page catalog. GeoSafari computer games, Mini-Museums, Mystery Rock, Exploring Ecology, Natural Collections, Mysteries of Light, Mysteries of Magnetism, Adventures in Science series has 12 different projects, Science Safari Stickers, Fantastic Cards on science subjects, Animal Big Books 14" x 20", Bug Viewers, Dino Checkers, Dino Tic Tac Toe.

EDUCATIONAL TEACHING AIDS
620 Lakeview Parkway, Vernon Hills, IL 60061 800-445-5985 Fax 800-ETA-9326 Email info@etauniverse.com http://www.etauniverse.com Retail Mail Order (Elementary School and Middle School)
Ask for 111-page K-12 science catalog filled with educational science materials and toys.

EDUCO INTERNATIONAL INC.
Contact Colleen Madsen 123 Cree Road, Sherwood Park, Alberta, Canada T8A 3X9 800-661-4142 403-467-9772 Fax 403-467-4014 Email mazes@educo.com http://www.educo.com Manufacturer (Preschool)
Ask for 20-page catalog. Manufacturer of quality bead-on-wire mazes. Science related portable mazes include Tyler Turtle, Roger Rocket, and Freddie Fish. Also Time Catcher, where kids collect treasures in their own time capsule.

ELENCO ELECTRONICS
150 W Carpenter, Wheeling, IL 60090 800-533-2441 847-541-3800
Fax 847-520-0085 Email elenco@elenco.com http://www.elenco.com
Manufacturer Retail Mail Order (Middle School to Adult)
Ask for catalog and brochure on Elenco Electronics Kits. Kits are designed for educational learning experiences for students and hobbyists. Many, but not all, of these kits require soldering.

ESTES INDUSTRIES
**Contact Ann Grimm   1295 H Street, Penrose, CO 81240
800-820-0202 Fax 800-820-0203 719-372-3217 Manufacturer
Retail to teachers. (High School to Adult)**
Ask for Estes Educator Catalog on school letterhead. Supplies model rockets, engines, accessories, and curricula.

Precision School Balance
Photo Courtesy of ETA

ETA
**620 Lakeview Pkwy, Vernon Hills, IL
60061-1838 800-445-5985
Fax 800-ETA-9326   847-816-5050
Fax 847-816-5066
http://www.etauniverse.com
Retail Mail Order
(Elementary School)**
Major supplier of educational toys and materials. Ask for 124-page ETA Science Catalog and 172-page ETA Math Catalog with supplies for the science classroom.

EXPLORATORIUM STORE
3601 Lyon St, San Francisco, CA 94123 415-561-0393
http://www.exploratorium.edu Retail Mail Order (All ages)
See web page that is filled with quality science toys and books, including the following toys: Megabubbles Kit, The Kaleidoscope Book and Kit, Zoetrope, Wild Wood, Magnetron, Gyros, Curiosity Box, Eagle Microscope, Mirage Maker, Micro-Bank, Erector Sets, Paradox 3-D Jigsaw Puzzle, and Ellipto.

EXPLORATOY
19560 S Rancho Way, Dominguez Hills, CA 90220 310-884-3490
800-995-9290 http://www.exploratoy.com Manufacturer Wholesale (Elementary School)
Ten-page catalog. Beakman's World Inquizator computerized quiz machine, Early Start learning machine, Critter Carnival insect house, Creature Catcher, The Antworks, Bug Pals, Riddle Rocks, Explorascope microscope, Test Tube Science in six science packs, Cosmic Observing Station telescope, Star Tower toy planetarium.

Levitron®
Photo Courtesy of Fascinations

FASCINATIONS TOYS & GIFTS,INC.

Toys Created by Physicists 19224 Des Moines Way So, Suite 100, Seattle, WA 98148 880-544-0810 206-870-3000 Fax 206-870-3004 Email fascinations@seanet.com http://www.fascinations.com Manufacturer Distributor Wholesale Retail Website Mail Order (Elementary School to High School) Ask for 8-page catalog. Well known science toys include Levitron, the antigravity top; Levitron accessories; Gyroring; MagnaSwing, Newton's cradle with magnets replacing balls; Magic Sand Wand; Astro-Blaster that works like a supernova; Micro Movie Viewers; and Dynamo, the kinetic flashlight that requires no batteries.

FRANK SCHAFFER PUBLICATIONS

23740 Hawthorne Blvd, Torrance, CA 90505 800-609-1735 Fax 800-837-7260 http://www.frankschaffer.com Manufacturer (Preschool to Elementary School)
Ask for 44-page Judy Instructo catalog. Judi Instructo, a division of Frank Schaffer Publications, offers Science Quest Kits on Earth, Weather, Light & Color, Magnets, Dinosaurs & Fossils, Insects, and Sound.

FREUD, MORRIS & WILLIAMS
**200 Fifth Ave, Suite 835, New York, NY 10010 Distributor
(Elementary School)**
Ask for 15-page catalog. Distributor of Science Tech microscopes, telescopes, binoculars, videoscope, anatomical models, magnets, periscopes, chemistry lab kit, magnifier, bug viewer, stereoscope, and more.

Videoscope Set
Photo Courtesy of
Freud, Morris & Williams

GEMINI KALEIDOSCOPES!
**128 McCarrell Lane, Zelienople, PA 16063   800-999-8700   724-452-8700
Fax 724-452-0867
Manufacturer Wholesale
(Elementary School to Adult)**
Ask for brochure. Toy kaleidoscopes handcrafted in U.S.A. Science kaleidoscopes include Bug Eye, Birds, Les Petites Fleurs, Nature Vision, and Kaleidosours.

Gemini Kaleidoscopes!
Photo Courtesy of
Gemini Kaleidoscopes

GEOCENTRAL

Contact Cindy Vader   1721 Action Ave, Napa, CA 94559
800-231-6083   707-224-7500   Fax 707-224-7400
Email cindy@geocentral.com Manufacturer Wholesale
(Elementary School to High School)
Quantity sets of rocks and minerals for retail sale. Flat boxes of mineral
and fossil assortments. Sea shell glow night lights. Agate bookends.
Ask for twenty four-page catalog.

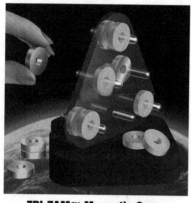

TRI-ZAM™ Magnetic Game
Photo Courtesy of Geospace Products

GEOSPACE PRODUCTS COMPANY

Contact Mitch Hamilton 1546 N W
Woodbine Way, Seattle, WA 98177
800-800-5090 206-365-5241
Fax 206-365-5241
Email debink@spingames.com
http://www.spingames.com
Manufacturer Wholesale and Retail
(Elementary School to Adult)
Magnetic marble toys, magnetic
levitation games, magnetic building
sets, and spin games, including Puzzle
Spin - M. C. Escher Collection.

GOOGOLPLEX TOY SYSTEMS INC.

195A Royal Crest Court, Markham, Ontario L3R 9X6 Canada
905-479-0064   905-447-0506   Fax 905-477-8891   Manufacturer
Wholesale.
Ask for brochure. The Googolplex Toy System is an educational
construction system than can be used to teach a wide variety of scientfic
topics.

GUIDECRAFT USA

P O Box 324/Industrial Center,
Garnerville, NY 10923-0324
800-544-6526 914-947-3500
Fax 914-947-3770
Email Gdcraft324@aol.com
Manufacturer Distributor
Retail Mail Order
(Preschool to Elementary School)
Ask for 16-page catalog. Fine wooden
toys that teach, including Clock Puzzle
House, Fax Machine, Mini-Animal
Puzzles, Time Sequencing, Wooden
Educational Games, 3-D Fruit &
Vegetable Puzzles, Career Sets, and Alligator Pull Toy.

Sorting & Counting Manipulatives
Photo Courtesy of Guidecraft USA

HOBERMAN DESIGNS, INC.

450 West 15th St, Suite 502, New York, NY 10011 888-229-3653
212-647-7656   Fax 212-647-7424   Email designs@hoberman.com
http://www.hoberman.com Manufacturer
(Elementary School to Adult)
Manufacturer of Hoberman Spheres that mechanically shrink and expand
by large factors.

HORTICULTURAL SALES PRODUCTS

505C Grand Caribe Isle, Coronado, CA   92118 888-ROOTVUE
619-423-9399   Fax 619-423-9398   Email rootvue@aol.com
http://members.aol.com/rootvue Manufacturer (Elementary School
to High School)
Manufacturer of Root-Vue-Farm: Watch carrots, radishes and onions
take form underground through a glass window. Other products include
Worm-Vue Wonders, Wonderfinders, Powersphere, and Naturestation.

Hugg-A-Planet®
Photo Courtesy of Hugg-A-Planet

HUGG-A-PLANET

Contact Patricia Howard 247 Rockingstone Ave, Larchmont, NY 10538 914-833-0200 Fax 914-833-0303 Email Hugaword@aol.com http://www.Hugg-A-Planet.com Manufacturer (Preschool to Elementary School)

Ask for brochure. Soft Earth globes and maps, including Hugg-A-Planet, Geophysical with no political boundaries, Hugg-America, Hugg-A-Star celestial sphere, and Hugg-A-Planet Mars.

HUNTAR CO.INC.

Contact Tammy Lawrence 473 Littlefield Ave, So. San Francisco, CA 94080 800-566-8686 650-873-8282 Fax 650-873-8292 Email Huntar.Magnet@worldnet.att.net Manufacturer Wholesale (Elementary School to High School)

Ask for 24-page catalog. Magnetic products include activity kits, wands, marbles, chips, shaped magnets, puzzle wheels, math & letter wheels, play boards, and floating rings.

I.G.C. GIOCATTOLI MAX SAS
Zona Instriale 43, Lanchiano, C H, Italy   0872-42205 Fax 0872-43281
Manufacturer Wholesale
(Elementary School to High School)
Ask for 44-page catalog.   Quality microscope kits, microscope monitors, gardening kits, chemistry sets, and telescopes.

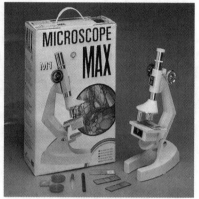

Microscope MAX   M1
Photo Courtesy of
I.G.C. Giocattoli MAX

IDEAL
A division of Tribune Education, P O Box 1650, Grand Rapids, MI 49501
800-845-8149 Fax 800-543-2690
http://www.ifair.com Manufacturer Retail Mail Order
(Elementary School)
Ask for 56-page teacher's catalog. Numerous products including science equipment.

Elementary Science Kit
Photo Courtesy of Ideal

IDEAL SCHOOL SUPPLY COMPANY
**11000 S Lavergne Ave, Oak Lawn, IL 60453 800-845-8149
http://www.ifair.com Distributor Retail Mail Order
(Preschool to Elementary School)**
Ask for the 50-page teacher catalog. Science measurement materials, chemistry experiment beakers and test tubes, equilateral prisms, physics pulleys, thermometers, classroom science kits, magnetic toys, natural science materials.

INSTANT PRODUCTS INC.
**Contact Jack Muenz-Winkler P O Box 33068, Louisville, KY 40232
800-862-6688   502-367-2266   Fax 502-368-6958   Manufacturer
(Elementary School to Adult)**
Manufacturer of capsules that dissolve into animal shapes in soft foam. For ages 5 years and above. Use these capsules to study the effect of temperature by dissolving capsules at different temperatures and measuring time variations.

IPI
**1758 N Park St, Suite B, Castle Rock, CO 80104 800-806-0023
303-688-1900   Fax   303-688-7936   http://www.ipitoys.com
Manufacturer Wholesale (Elementary School)**
Manufacturer of NASA licensed toys.

JCS, INC.

P O Box 12455, Chicago, IL 60612
800-469-6653 312-226-5772
Fax 312-226-5774   Manufacturer
Distributor Wholesale
(Elementary School to Adult)
Ask for brochure. Voyage Earth labs include Volcano Adventure, Earthquake Explorer, Tornado Adventure, and Geyser Exploration. Weird Monster Science includes Shrink Putty, Power Surge, Rocket Flight Formula, Invisible Ink, Flying Things and Slime Conversion Potion. Crafty Kids series includes Foot Prints, Scribble, and Face Kit.

Eruption
The Volcano Adventure Lab
Photo Courtesy of JCS

KLUTZ

455 Portage Ave, Palo Alto, CA 94306-2213 800-558-8944
Fax 800-524-4075 650-424-0739 Manufacturer Retail Mail Order
(Elementary School to High School)
Ask for the 46-page Klutz Catalogue. Really fun toys and novelties. Amazon Worms, Smartballs, Smartrings, The Explorabook - a kids science museum in a book, ExploraCenter, Backyard Weather Station kit, Mega-Magnet Set, Backyard Bird Book with bird caller, The Aerobie Orbiter, Rubber Stamp Bug Kit, Vinyl Vermin, Kids Gardening Guide, World Record Paper Airplane Kit, The Arrowcopter, Megaballoons, Bubble Book, Zoetrope, juggling materials.

KOLBE CONCEPTS, INC.

P O Box 15667, Phoenix, AZ 85060 602-840-9770 Fax 602-952-2706
http://www.kolbe.com **Manufacturer Retail (All ages)**
Ask for brochure. Think-ercises, Glop Shop - inventor's assortment, Go
Power - science experiments, Using Your Senses, Solar Power Winners
- experiment book, Decide & Design - inventor's book.

KOPLOW GAMES, INC.

**369 Congress St, Boston, MA 02210 800-899-0711 617-482-4011
Fax 617-482-3423 Manufacturer (Elementary School to Adult)**
Ask for 28-page catalog. Manufacturer of dice and dice games, including
numbered dice of all shapes for math and science. Action Fractions is an
activity for teaching fractions ages 7 and up. Sandtimers, pawns, bells,
chips, stickers, rubber dice, glow-in-the-dark dice, and glass stones.

Space Age Crystal Growing Kit
Photo Courtesy of Kristal Educational

KRISTAL EDUCATIONAL INC.

**Distributed by Ira Cooper, Inc., P O
Box 2137, Woodinville, WA 98072
206-720-6264 Fax 206-720-6317
http://www.mysteriousart.com
Distributor Wholesale
(Elementary School to High School)**
Ask for 26-page catalog. Mineral
crystal growing kits, including Space
Age Crystal Kits; Crystal Spheres,
Pyramids & Jewelry; Crystal Caves;
Dab'a'Dino (Paintable stuffed
dinosaurs); National Geographic
Society's Expedition Series; Gem Tree
Kits; Archeology Kits; and more.

LAKESHORE LEARNING MATERIALS
2695 E Dominguez St, Carson, CA 90749 800-428-4414
Fax 310-537-5403 http://www.lakeshorelearning.com
Manufacturer and Distributor Retail   (Elementary School)
Ask for 200-page catalog. The catalog of this major distributor of
learning materials has eight pages of science materials.

LAWRENCE HALL OF SCIENCE
University of California, Berkeley, CA 94720-5200   510-642-1016
Fax 510-642-1055   Email lhsstore@uclink4.berkeley.edu
http://www.lhs.berkeley.edu
See web site filled with books, teachers' and parents' guides, science kits,
videos, and ordering instructions. Known as Eureka!: Teaching Tools
from the Lawrence Hall of Science.

LEAPFROG
Contact Scott Masline 1250 45th St,
Suite 150, Emeryville, CA   94608
800-701-532 510-595-2470
Fax 510-595-2478
Email scottm@leapfrogtoys.com
http://www.leapfrogtoys.com
Manufacturer Wholesale
(Elementary School)
Ask for catalog. Science toys include
National Geographic Really Wild
Animals, an interactive electronic
talking toy, and Space Explorer
Shuttle, a toy that talks when cards are
inserted, teaching hundreds of facts
about astronomy and space.

**National Geographic
Real Wild Animals**
Photo Courtesy of Leapfrog

Puppet Forest

Photo Courtesy of Learning Resources

LEARNING RESOURCES, INC.

Contact Lisa Hoffmann   380 N Fairway Drive, Vernon Hills, IL 60061   800-222-3909   847-573-8400   Fax 847-573-8425   http://www.learningresources.com   **Manufacturer Wholesale (Preschool and Elementary School)**

Exceptional range of award-winning educational toys. Ask for 72-page catalog. Pretend & Play Calculator Cash Register, math and science measurement materials, geometry shapes, base ten products, thermometers, Power of Science line of science accessories, Idea Factory Science Kits, the Investigator Slide Viewer with slide strip sets, the Quantum Big Screen Microscope.

LEGO DACTA - THE EDUCATIONAL DIVISION OF LEGO SYSTEMS, INC.

555 Taylor Rd, P. O. Box 1600, Enfield, CN 06083-1600 800-527-8339 **Manufacturer Retail and Wholesale Distributed by PITSCO 800-362-4308 (Elementary School to High School)**

Gear, lever and pulley toys, Technic classroom kits, Technic control centers, teacher's guide books, Pneumatics, Logowriter Robotics for Apple and MS-DOS, Control Lab for Apple and MS-DOS.

LIFE-LIKE PRODUCTS
1600 Union Ave, Baltimore, MD
21211-1998 410-554-9470
Fax 410-235-6887 **Manufacturer**
Wholesale (Elementary School)
Manufacturer of Darda motorized cars
and track sets.

Ultra Speed™
Turbo Power Speedway
Photo Courtesy of Life-Like Products

LIGHTRIX, INC.
2132 Adams Ave, San Leandro, CA 94577 800-850-4656
510-577-7800 Fax 415-244-9795 Email dlr@lightrix.com
http://www.lightrix.com **Manufacturer Wholesale (Elementary**
School to Adult)
Holographic toys and novelties. Products include bright holograms of
nature & science, holographic sunglasses, Spectrix Visors, Eccentrix
diffraction discs, science puzzles, dinosaurs, and more.

M. RUSKIN CO.

P O Box 222, Rockaway Park, NY 11694 718-474-1680
Fax 718-474-5439 **Manufacturer Wholesale (Elementary School)**
Ask for brochure. Educational place mats including science subjects.

**Magnets - Magnetic Wand
Activity Kit**
Photo Courtesy of The Magnet Source

THE MAGNET SOURCE

Master Magnetics, Inc., 607 Gilbert
St, Castle Rock, CO 80104
800-874-6248 303-688-3966
Fax 303-688-5303
Email magsales@magnetsource.com
http://www.magnetsource.com
**Manufacturer Wholesale
(Elementary School to Adult)**
Ask for catalog. Magnetic kits, toys,
and educational products, including
magnetic balls, wands, Discovery Kits,
Earth globes, tape, and more.

MATTEL, INC.

333 Continental Blvd, El Segundo, CA 90245-5012 310-252-3520
Fax 310-252-4592 **Manufacturer (Elementary School)**
Manufacturer of Hot Wheels and Hot Wheels track sets.

MAYFLOWER DEVELOPMENT AND TRADING CORP.
P O Box 705, Bellevue, WA 98009 425-747-7766 Fax 425-957-9384
Emailswitchon@concentric.nethttp://www.concentric.net/~switchon
Manufacturer Wholesale Retail Mail Order
(Elementary School to High School)
Manufacturer of Switch On!: Innovative Electronic Building Blocks.
Have fun setting up easy-to-connect, safe circuit blocks to switch on: a
light bulb, a fire engine, a flashing door bell, an electric fan, or create
your own circuit. An excellent, fun way to teach electrical circuits to
children.

MEADE INSTRUMENTS CORP.
6001 Oak Canyon, Irvine, CA 92620-4205 949-451-1450
Fax   949-451-1460   http://www.meade.com   Manufacturer
Distributor (Elementary School to College)
Ask for 102-page catalog. Quality optical telescopes, binoculars, and
spotting scopes.

MINDWARE
2720 Patton Rd, Roseville, MN 55113-1138 800-999-0398
Fax 888-299-9273 Retail Mail Order (All Ages)
Ask for 40-page catalog. Products include many science toys, puzzles,
and games.

MORE BALLS THAN MOST

Contact Virginia Wages-Plotkin 26 W 17th St, # 702, New York, NY 10011 800-544-3688, ext 13 212-691-9660, ext 13 Fax 212-691-9633 Email Virginia@MBTMNY.mhs.compuserve.com **Manufacturer Distributor Wholesale (Elementary School to Adult)**

Ask for 20-page catalog. Toys include hot air balloon kits, The Rokit (launch a soda bottle up to 50 feet with compressed air), Buster Bloodvessel (wooden and wire puzzles), Optical (pocket optical illusion jigsaw), Penultimate (a pen that floats on air and spins on a frictionless bed), juggling supplies, and more.

MUSEUM PRODUCTS

84 Route 27, Mystic, CT 06355 800-395-5400 203-538-6433 Distributor Retail Mail Order (Elementary School to High School)

Ask for 56-page catalog. Unique toys and educational products from science and nature.

Nature Print® Paper
Photo Courtesy of
Natureprint Paper Products

NATUREPRINT PAPER PRODUCTS

P O Box 314, Moraga, CA 94556 Manufacturer (Elementary School to High School)

Natureprint paper and transparencies. This sun-sensitive paper exposes in direct sunlight to create white on blue prints of leaf outlines or animal picture transparencies. Expose for 2-3 minutes and then develop in tap water in seconds.

ORBIX CORPORATION
6329 Mori Street, McLean, VA 22101 703-356-0695 Manufacturer (Elementary School to Adult)
Ask for brochure. Manufacturer of Odd Balls, an educational toy made from three types of wedges assembled onto a central disk. You can use Odd Balls to demonstrate principles of geometry and physics and to teach mathematics concepts including fractions. They reassemble to make tops, pinwheels, and balls.

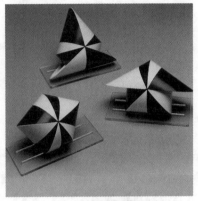

Odd Balls®
Photo Courtesy of Orbix

OWI INCORPORATED
Contact Craig Morioka   1160 Mahalo Place, Compton, CA 90220-5443 310-638-4732 Fax 310-638-8347
Email owi@ix.netcom.com   http://www.owirobot.com
Manufacturer Wholesale   (Nine Years to Adult)
Ask for brochure on Robotics and for information on retail distributors. This manufacturer makes several different robotic kits requiring different levels of assembly sophistication. The new Triple Action Solar Car Kit allows batteries or solar power with a multi-speed transmission.

PARADISE CREATIONS
**21789 Town Place Dr, Boca Raton, FL 33433 Contact Phil Seltzer,
11806 Gorham Ave #7, Los Angeles, CA 90049 310-207-4451
Fax 310-207-6320 Manufacturer Distributor
(Elementary School to High School)**
Ask for brochure. Fully articulated human anatomy skeletons that easily
snap together, including The Skull, 14-inch and 23-inch Skeletons, Male
Skeleton, Female Skeleton, and Bones-Organs-Muscles. Also Seashell
Collector Sets.

PHYSICS OF TOYS DEMONSTRATION SET # 71938-02
$ 165.00   PHYSICS FUN AND DEMONSTRATIONS
MANUAL # 58225 $ 13.50 CENCO
**3300 Cenco Parkway, Franklin Park, IL 60131-1364 800-262-3626
Fax 800-814-0607 http://www.cenconet.com Retail (All ages)**
This set of 23 familiar toys demonstrate physical principles as explained
in the accompanying manual.

**PITSCO Rooster
Remote Control Robot**
Photo Courtesy of PITSCO

PITSCO
**1002 E Adams, P O Box 1708,
Pittsburg, KS 66762-1708
800-835-0686 800-358-4983
http://www.pitsco.com
Fax 800-533-8104 Manufacturer
Distributor Retail Mail Order
(Elementary School to College)**
Ask for 432-page catalog. Major
distributor of science materials,
including books, new science toys,
video, and more. Over 600 new
products.

PLAY-BY-PLAY ACE-ACME
4100 Forest Park, St. Louis, MO 63108-2899   800-325-7888
http://www.pbpus.com Importer, Manufacturer and Distributor
Retail Mail Order (All ages)
Ask for 110-page catalog filled with a very large variety of inexpensive toys and novelties that demonstrate natural phenomena. An excellent source for science teachers.

RAMONA ENTERPRISES, INC.
80 Apparel Way, San Francisco, CA
94124   800-RAMONA-5
415-695-0200   Fax 415-695-0238
Manufacturer Wholesale
(Elementary   School   to   Middle
School)
Ask for brochure. Manufacturer of Gear-O-Matic, a toy that teaches how gears change speeds, forces, and motions.   Purchase   on   school letterhead.

Gear-O-Matic
Photo Courtesy of Ramona Enterprises

Cosmic Observer 50x Telescope
Photo Courtesy of
Science & Nature Distributors

SCIENCE & NATURE DISTRIBUTORS

A division of Downeast Concepts, Inc., 20 Downeast Drive, Yarmouth, ME 04096 800-344-5555 Fax 800-457-7087 Customer Service 888-273-0946 Distributor Wholesale (Elementary School)

Ask for 88-page catalog. Large variety of science toys, games, books, and lab equipment. Product categories include space & flight, earth science, life science, physical science, science kits, brain games, novelties, books, posters, and lab equipment.

SCIENTIFIC EXPLORER, INC.

4020 E Madison, Suite 326, Seattle, WA 98112 800-900-1182 206-322-7611 Fax 206-322-7610 Email sciex@scientificexplorer.com http://www.scientificexplorer.com http://www.gettoys.com Manufacturer Retail Mail Order (Elementary School to Adult)

Ask for 16-page catalog. Manufacturer of science and adventure kits including Fun with Your Cat, Fun with Your Dog, Smithsonian Adventures Series, Aerial Camera, High Altitude Launcher, Science of Scent, Make Animal Soaps, Kitchen Science, Educational Cooking Center, Nature Adventures, Exploring Electronics, Science of Sound, and many more.

SELSI COMPANY, INC.

P O Box 10, 194 Greenwood Ave, Midland Park, NJ 07432-0010
800-275-7357   201-612-9200   Fax 201-612-9548   Manufacturer
Wholesale (Elementary School to Adult)

Quality binoculars, telescopes, student microscope sets, magnifiers, toy
kaleidoscopes, glass prisms, student magnets, compasses, barometers,
altimeters, metal detectors.

SKY PUBLISHING CORP. CATALOG

Sky Publishing Corp., 49 Bay State Rd, Cambridge, MA 02138 / Sky
& Telescope, P O Box 9111, Belmont, MA 02178-9111 800-253-0245
617-864-7360   Fax 617-864-6117   Email skytel@skypub.com
http://www.skypub.com Since 1941. (High School to College)

Ask for 32-page catalog of products for professional and amateur
astronomers. Products include maps, books, videos, globes, posters,
software, CD-ROMs, slide sets, star atlases, and planispheres.

SMALL WORLD TOYS

5711 Buckingham Parkway, Culver City, CA 90230 800-421-4153
310-645-9680   Fax 310-410-9606   Manufacturer   Distributor
Wholesale (Preschool and Elementary School)

Gyroscopes, Gravity Graph, inflatable globes, Backyard Scientist, mineral
sets, Bug World, dinosaur skeleton kits, Polyopticon optical toy kits, Bug
Hotel, magnetic toys, Gigantic Glow Stars, dinosaur models, origami kits,
Whirlybirds, Newton's Yo-Yo, Finger Tops, Astronaut Food, animal sets,
magnifier toys, Sparkling Wheels, Relaxable Globe Balls.

SOMERVILLE HOUSE

3080 Yonge St, Suite 5000, Toronto, Ontario, Canada M4N 3N1
800-387-9776 Fax 800-260-9777 416-488-5938 Fax 416-488-5506
Email sombooks@goodmedia.com   http://www.sombooks.com
Manufacturer Distributor Wholesale (Elementary School)
Ask for 32-page catalog. The Bones Book with plastic skeleton, dinosaur
books with plastic skeletons, The Environmental Detective Kit. Books
packaged with toy models. Also The Bug Book & Bottle, The Ultimate
Science Kit, Snail Tongues and Spider Fangs, Bug Eyes and Butterfly
Wings, Coral Reef, Birds of Prey, Insects and Spiders, Snakes and
Lizards, and more.

Two Potato Clock
Photo Courtesy of Summit Learning

SUMMIT LEARNING

P O Box 493, Ft. Collins, CO 80522
800-777-8817
http://www.youngexplorers.summitl
earning.com   Retail Mail Order
(Elementary School)
Ask for Science Manipulatives Catalog,
Math Manipulatives Catalog, and
Young Explorers Catalog. These
catalogs are filled with educational
materials for math and science
including the following categories:
Linear Tools; Volume and Capacity;
Weights and Measures; Time and
Temperature; Problem-Solving; Estimation; Graphs; Probability; Earth
Science; Astronomy; Science and Nature, and more.

SUN-MATE CORP.
8223 Remmet Ave, Canoga Park, CA 91304 818-883-7766
Fax 818-883-8171 http://www.sun-mate.com
Manufacturer Wholesale (Elementary School)
Science educational solar toys, wooden motor kits, adventure kits, and
more.

TASCO
2889 Commerce Parkway, Miramar, FL 33025 / P O Box 269000,
Pembroke Pines, FL 33026 888-GET-TASCO 954-252-3600
Fax 954-252-3705 http://www.tascosales.com
Manufacturer Distributor (Elementary School to Adult)
Ask for 52-page Recreational Optics catalog. Quality optical products for
all ages. Children's products include Big Screen Microscope, Binoculars,
Periscopes, Magnifiers and more. Adult products include Lasersite
Rangefinder, Night Watch Viewing Optics, Binoculars, Zoom Binoculars,
Sport Telescopes, Astronomical Telescopes, and more.

TEACHER CREATED MATERIALS, INC.
Contact Steve Mitchell 6421 Industry Way, Westminster, CA 92683
714-891-2273 Fax 714-892-0283 Email alacola@teachercreated.com
http://www.teachercreated.com Manufacturer Wholesale Retail
Mail Order (Elementary School)
Ask for catalogs: Teacher Created Materials, Techworks, Curriculum
Catalog, and Professional Developmental Seminars. Their goal is to help
teachers keep up with new educational trends. Thematic Teaching
Resources includes Weather, Human Body, Space/Solar System, and
Ancient Civilizations. Techworks helps teachers use whatever hardware
and software they have to teach the existing curriculum more effectively.

Junior Computer Gold
Photo Courtesy of Team Concepts

TEAM CONCEPTS NORTH AMERICA, LTD

331 Eisenhower Lane South, Lombard, IL 60148 630-261-0661 Fax 630-261-0696 http://www.team-concepts.com **Manufacturer Wholesale (Preschool School to Middle School)** Manufacturer of electronic learning aids. Numerous products are available and each resembles a lap top computer.

TESSELATIONS

688 W 1st St, Suite 5, Tempe, AZ 85281 800-655-5341 602-967-7455 Fax 602-967-7582 Email tessella@futureone.com http://tesselations.com **Manufacturer Wholesale Retail Mail Order (Elementary School to Adult)** Ask for 8-page catalog. Puzzles that creatively combine math, art and fun, including Monkey Business; Spin, Rock & Roll, a 3-D puzzle that creates tops, pendulums, balls, and more; Tessel-Gons; Tessel-Gon Stars; Tessellation Kaleidoscope; Tangrams; Captured Worlds, panoramic projections on polyhedra; and many more. Classroom kits available.

TOY-RRIFIC, INC.

944 E 4th St, Los Angeles, CA 90013 888-869-7743 Fax 213-617-7502 **Distributor Wholesale (Elementary School)** Ask for catalog. Science toys distributed include microscope, Wildlife Study Set, and Super-Super Balls.

TRIOPS, INC.
Educational Science Products, P O Box 10852, Pensacola, FL 32524
800-200-3466   850-479-4415   Fax 850-479-3315   Manufacturer
Distributor Wholesale (Elementary School to High School)
Ask for brochures and catalogs. Products include Instant Triops (eggs of
this prehistoric creature hatch in water in 24 hours), Zooplankton, Instant
Daphnia, Instant Killifish, Instant Green Algae, Instant Brine Shrimp, and
more.

UNCLE MILTON INDUSTRIES, INC.
5717 Corsa Ave, Westlake Village,
CA 91362-4001   800-869-7555
818-707-0800   Fax 818-707-0878
Email antfarm@ix.netcom.com
http://www.unclemilton.com
Manufacturer Wholesale
(Elementary School)
Seven-page catalog contains Ant Farms
(Milton Levine invented the Ant Farm
in 1956), Pocket Museums, Fossil
Hunt, Krazy Klowns, Light-Up Critter
City, BugJug, Star Theater home
planetarium,   Super   GeoScope

Surf Frogs™
Photo Courtesy of
Uncle Milton Industries

microscope, Hydro Greenhouse, Rock & Mineral Hunt, Surf Frogs. Surf
Frogs is a live frog habitat where frogs grow from tadpoles.

USTOY CONSTRUCTIVE PLAYTHINGS

1227 E 119th St, Gradview, MO 64030-1117 800-448-4115
816-761-5900   Fax 816-761-9295   Email ustoy@ustoyco.com
http://www.ustoyco.com Manufacturer Distributor Wholesale
Retail Mail Order (Preschool to Elementary School)
Ask for 200-page catalog filled with educational fun for the preschool and
elementary school age child including six pages of hands-on science
materials.

U - ME®
Photo Courtesy of
Van Cort Instruments

VAN CORT INSTRUMENTS, INC.

12 Greenfield Rd, P O Box 215,
South Deerfield, MA 01373-0215
800-432-2678 413-586-9800
Fax 413-665-2300
Email sales@vancort.com
http://www.vancort.com
Manufacturer Wholesale   Retail
Mail Order
(Elementary School to Adult)
Ask for catalog. Manufacturer of
quality   telescopes,   kaleidoscopes,
timepieces, magnifying glasses, and
unique instruments including the toy, U-ME, an optical illusion mirror
that combines faces. Products handmade in New England.

WESTMINSTER INTERNATIONAL CO., INC.
436 Armour Circle N E, Atlanta, GA   30324 800-241-8697
404-876-6008   Fax 404-892-3471   Email toys@compuserve.com
http://www.westminsterinc.com   Manufacturer Distributor
Wholesale (Elementary School)
Ask for 16-page catalog. Fast action, fun toys including Diving Dophin, Galactic Shooter, Handboilers, Pen Boilers, Liquid Motion, Color Wave, Sandtimer, Magic Illusion Disk, Newton's Cradles, and more.

THE WILD GOOSE COMPANY
375 Whitney Ave, 375 W 1455 S, Salt Lake City, UT 84115
800-373-1498 801-466-1172 Fax 801-466-1186
http://www.widgoosescience.com
Manufacturer Retail Mail Order (Elementary School)
Ask for 16-page catalog. Science materials include Newton's Apple Kits, Teacher Books, Megalab kits, T-Shirts, Posters, Professional Development Training, and Student-Centered Programs.

Supersonic Ear®
Photo Courtesy of Wild Planet Toys

WILD PLANET TOYS
Contact Molly McCahan 98 Battery Street, Suite 300, San Francisco, CA 94111 800-247-6570 415-705-8300 Fax 415-705-8311
Email mccahan@wildplanet.com
http://www.wildplanet.com
Manufacturer (Elementary School to Middle School)
Wild Planet Toys manufacture a series of fun investigative toys demonstrating that technology is simply an extension of the human body for observation and communication.   Toys   include Electronic Gaget Set, Hands-Free Walkie Talkie, Radio Watch, Night Scope Binoculars, Wrist Talkies, Body Mike, Signal Watch, Sonic Scope, Metal Detector, Sleuth Scope, Supersonic Ear, and many more.

WIT CRAFTS
50 Main St, Malden, MA 02148 781-324-0114 Fax 781-322-7208
Email jqshan@aol.com Manufacturer Wholesale (All Ages)
Ask for brochure. Hand-made, mahogany-wood novelty items that are both inspiring art and witty entertainment. Science items include Rolling Balls, Jigsaw Puzzles, Trees with Birds and Monkeys, Animals Set, Dinosaurs Set, Gears & Dial, and more.

Y AND B ASSOCIATES

33 Primrose Lane, Hempstead, New York 11550 516-481-0256
Fax 516-481-0256 Manufacturer
(Elementary School to Middle School)
Manufacturer of Archi-Forms (a model and construction kit for the exloration of physical space), Newton's Run (25 feet of tubing for flexible marble runs), and Puzzabilities (create your own optical illusions).

ZOMETOOL

1526 South Pearl Street, Denver, CO
80210 888-966-3386 303-733-2880
Fax 303-733-3116
Email sales@zometool.com
http://www.zometool.com
Manufacturer
(Elementary School to Adult)
The Zome System is a versatile, creative construction toy used by mathematicians, scientists, engineers and architects. Yet, it is perfect as a classroom teaching tool as well as creative play. The various possible

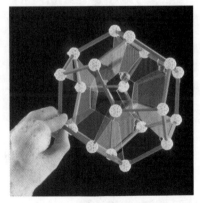

Zome System™
Photo Courtesy of Zometool

construction angles reflect the forces of physics and nature. Teacher kits, student kits, researcher kits, and lesson plans available.

Index

About the Author

Thomas W. Sills has been associated with Wright College, one of the City Colleges of Chicago, since 1989, and with the City Colleges since 1981. He has held several teaching positions over the years and has worked on course and lab development. He currently holds the position of professor of physical science.

His diverse professional career in science education includes test development, science toy design, science teacher training, reviewing college physics textbooks, and acting as science consultant to programs for the gifted. He is also faculty coordinator of telecourses on Channel 20/Chicago educational television, including *The Mechanical Universe* and *Planet Earth.*

In high school he received an award at the International Science Fair for his student science project on learning and memory. In 1967 he taught college physical science for elementary teachers as his first teaching assignment. In 1977 he received his Ph.D. in physics and education at Purdue University.

Dr. Sills is a serious collector of books and manuscripts on science and technology. But most of all, he enjoys going to new places to meet new people in order to stimulate ideas. "Doing adventuresome things is just plain fun."